(WALES)

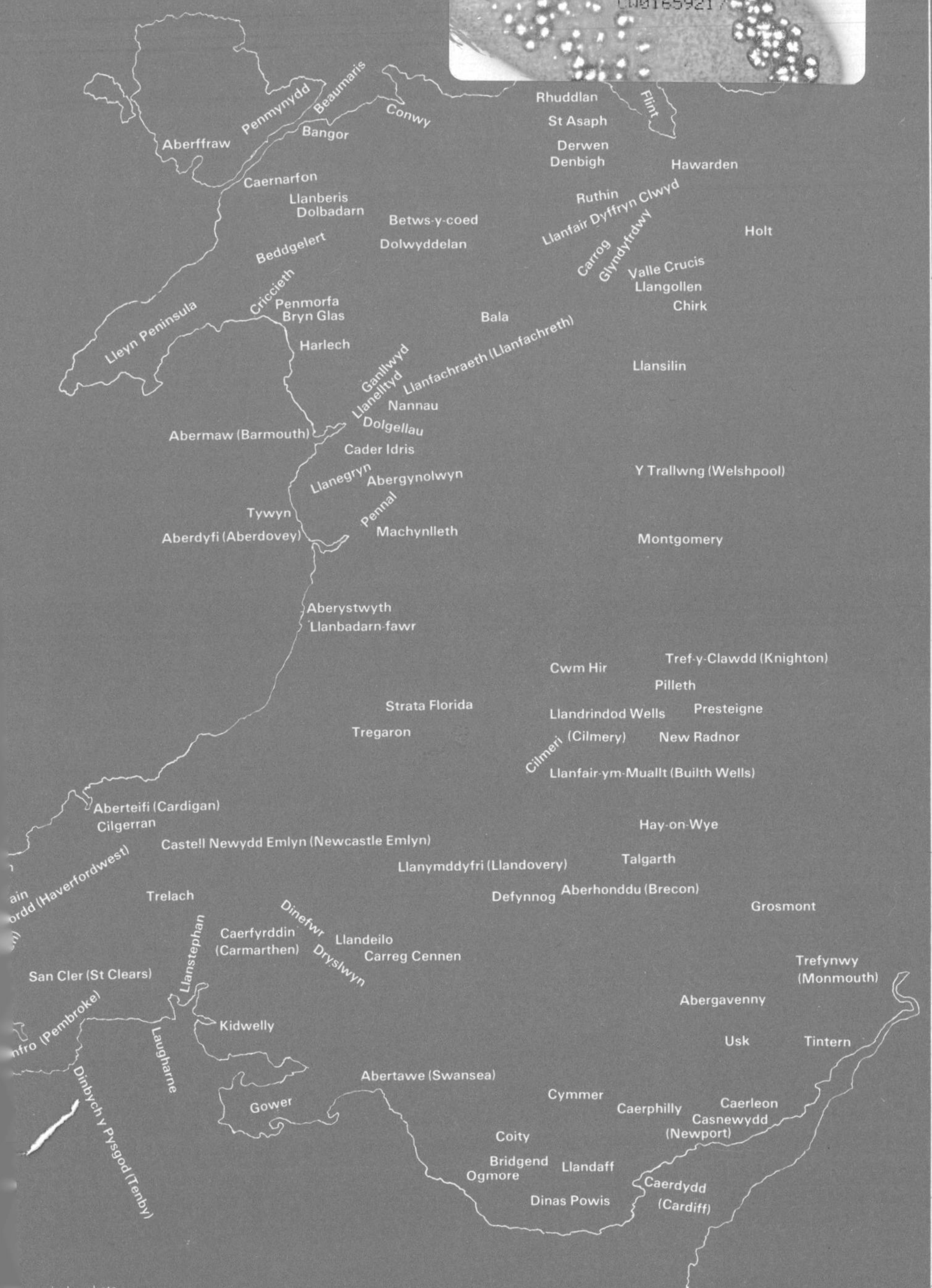

own in brackets.

INSURRECTION IN WALES

INSURRECTION IN WALES

The rebellion of the Welsh led by Owen Glyn Dwr (Glendower) against the English Crown in 1400

by

D. HELEN ALLDAY

TERENCE DALTON LIMITED
LAVENHAM . SUFFOLK
1981

Published by
TERENCE DALTON LIMITED
LAVENHAM . SUFFOLK

ISBN 0 86138 001 0

Text Photoset in 11/12pt. Baskerville

Printed in Great Britain at
THE LAVENHAM PRESS LIMITED
LAVENHAM . SUFFOLK

Contents

Index of Illustrations

All photographs, unless otherwise stated, by the author.

Preface and Acknowledgements

SEVERAL eminent Welsh scholars have written detailed accounts of this turbulent period in their country's history. Others have preseved their literary inheritance and culture at times when their endeavours were regarded with some hostility. As an Englishwoman I acknowledge the great debt I owe to their diligence.

In writing this book I have attempted to unravel the confusing genealogies, and inconsistent loyalties, of medieval families both Royal and "common" – English and Welsh. If, as a result of reading the story of Owen Glyn Dwr, the reader feels that he has reached some understanding of the conflict between two closely-linked nationalities, then I believe that my own small contribution will have been worthwhile.

During my travels all over Wales I met so many anonymous men and women who assisted me in so many ways, from castle custodians to local farmers and shopkeepers, I am indebted to them. Many Welsh people have assisted my efforts, and I am grateful to all those who did not think that my ambition to compile a history of their Glyn Dwr was too presumptuous, especially as many of my friends in Wales are the descendants of those who fought on one side, or on the other.

My thanks are due particularly to Mr John Elwyn Evans, Mrs M. Jones and Mrs Gwyneth Hancock of Llyfrgell Sir Feirionnydd, Merioneth County Library, Dolgellau whose encouragement and active assistance considerably eased my way during many months of research and preparation. I thank also the Merioneth Archives Service at Penarlag, Dolgellau.

I am grateful to Dr Robert Haworth, whose constructive advice and technical information were invaluable. My sincere thanks are due to my publishers, without whose guidance, great kindness and experience this book would not have been possible.

To my family, who deserve the highest commendation for their patience and forbearance, I can only express my deep gratitude.

I am indebted to everyone whose faith in my ability to complete the task never wavered, and hope that I have not failed them.

D. Helen Allday.
Abermaw
Gwynedd
July, 1980.

*   *   *   *   *

To my mother and father

Introduction

IN ENGLISH Literature, the name "Glendower" appears only as a character in *Henry IV, Part One* by William Shakespeare, or as an off-stage player, or as a wandering spirit in romantic poetry. These references to some obscure Welshman are largely ignored by the majority of readers, mostly schoolchildren, who are naturally more concerned with the history of their own tribe rather than with the story of Wales. History books often ignore Glendower completely, since he was a rebel, and ultimately unsuccessful in his struggle against Henry IV and the young man who later became the glorious Henry V.

Yet the name of Glendower still stirs latent feelings of patriotism in Welsh hearts even after so many centuries. This minor Shakespearian character, too often portrayed as a fourteenth century Merlin, is no mythical wizard but Owen Glyn Dwr, the great leader, ranking alongside Llywelyn the Great and all those other "rebels" who sought to drive the English out of their country. National heroes are rare beings, and their exploits deserve publicity. Only by revealing the deeds of exceptional leaders, and by examining the effects of those deeds on ordinary people, can we begin to understand our own emotions and reactions when national pride is discussed.

Paradoxically, while major European countries attempt to unite, small countries such as Scotland, Ireland and Wales are seeking to establish separate identities. This national pride is a powerful emotion which can drive men and women to commit acts they would not otherwise even contemplate. The English find it difficult to understand why these countries, uneasily welded into one Great Britain, feel so strongly about their ancestors, cultures and languages. The history of England has been preserved in minute detail; heroes have been praised and great battles have been marked by monuments. As the victors the English have never felt the need to insist on recognition; even defeats have become honourable, and English supremacy has been acknowledged without conscious effort. Although many of the heroes and heroines who were involved in early episodes were not strictly "English", their names have become synonymous with English valour.

The history of neighbouring Wales is not generally taught in English schools, except as an afterthought. The arrogance is probably unintentional. To me, Owen Glyn Dwr is as fascinating a hero as any leader who has emerged in Britain. His story has helped me to understand the new surge of patriotism that compels a nation to seek independence and to preserve a language and a culture which were disappearing rapidly. As I have travelled around this lovely country, experiencing all seasons and elements, following ancient tracks, visiting crumbling castles and tracing the routes of invading armies, my admiration for those who fought to free their homeland has increased with each journey. There are some who will maintain that Glyn Dwr was not a patriot at all, but a Welsh baron fighting for his lost estates, and an Anglicised Welshman at that. Yet such a motive cannot embrace all the facts. You can decide for yourself. Owen Glyn Dwr has earned a place in the hearts of Welsh people; he deserves a place in the history of Britain.

Students of Shakespeare's History Plays may find this story helpful as background material, and I hope that others will be stimulated to read again those plays which were so often incomprehensible at school because the events and places were unfamiliar.

The name of this"Valiant Prince" is given variously as Owen Glyn Dwr, Owain Glyndwr or Owen Glendower.

Sir J. E. Lloyd's guidance has been followed in this text, although many Welsh people would probably prefer the use of Owain rather than Owen. Glendower of course is the Anglicised version of a difficult Welsh name — just as Shakespeare used "Fleullen" in *Henry V* to represent the Welsh: Llywelyn. For the sake of clarity it should be pointed out that the Welsh names are written in the original form whenever possible, but these are pronounced simply as:
Tudor — Tudur; Tewdwr.
Meredith — Maredudd.
Griffith — Gruffydd; Gruffudd.

Rees — Rhys.
David — Dafydd.
Howel — Hywel.
William — Gwilym.

Today we tend to forget that before the Angles and Saxons invaded these islands, the inhabitants were mainly from one or other of the many Celtic tribes such as the Iceni and their queen, Boadicea, which settled in East Anglia. Now there is a growing awareness of our past and an appreciation that Welsh, the oldest living cultural language in Europe, must, understandably, be encouraged to survive. One Celtic branch settled in Brittany, England and Wales and were called Brythoniaid, Britons. Their language split into three tongues: Welsh, Cornish and Breton. Cornish fell out of common use in the eighteenth century although many words survive particularly in house and place names and a small but dedicated group of Cornishmen are trying to revive the tongue of their forefathers. Breton onion sellers can still understand, and be understood by, Welshmen in these present times.

Increased interest in the Welsh language has led to a gradual change back to the spelling of place names and this provides problems for many non-Welsh speaking people. To obtain some standardisation for this book I have used two easily available maps, Wales Tourist Map 1978 published by the Wales Tourist Board, Cardiff (Caerdydd), and Sheet 7, Wales and the West Midlands in the Routemaster Series of Great Britain published by Ordnance Survey, Southampton, Spring 1978. Welsh names are used but when there is an Anglicised version it follows, in brackets afterwards, at its first appearance where one or the other or both are shown on the maps. In some instances the Anglicised name has been dropped completely; for instance there is no longer Caernarvon since there is no V in the 28-letter Welsh alphabet. It is Caernarfon. The Ordnance Survey book, *Place Names on Maps of Scotland and Wales* provides a pronunciation guide and a glossary which helps in translating place names, always descriptive, into English. In Wales there are many books available for the visitor, including *Speak Welsh* by Gwen Pritchard Jones, an introduction to the language published by John Jones Cardiff Ltd, and *Welsh Place-names and Their Meanings* by Dewi Davies printed by the Cambrian News, Aberystwyth.

In April 1974 eight new and larger counties were formed

from the old thirteen counties of Wales. In this book the old county names have been used and the new county name of which it forms a part follows in brackets in the first instance. For ease of reference there is a list of places with the Welsh name and its Anglicised version where one exists, and a list of the old and new counties at the end of this book.

* * * * *

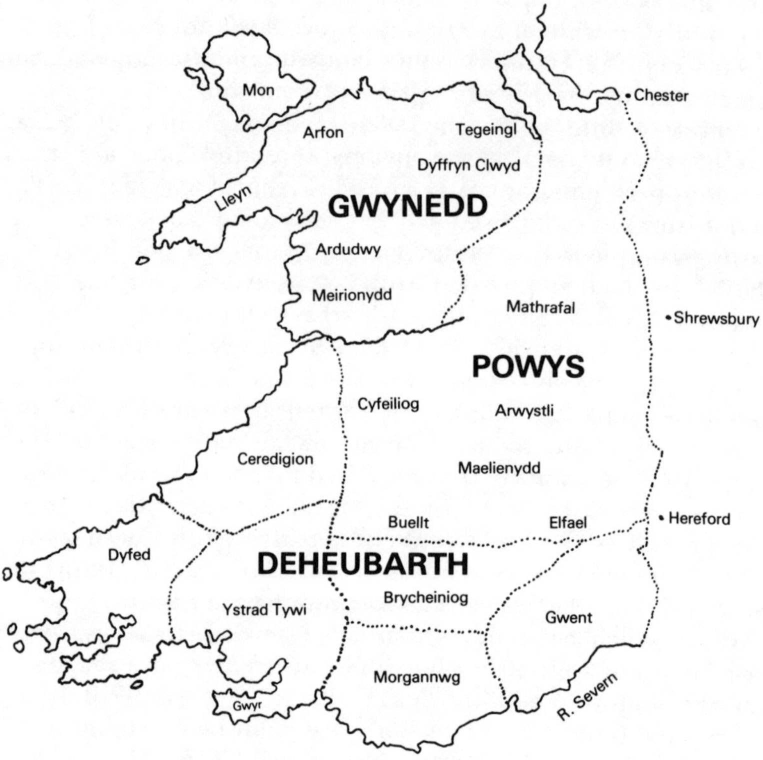

WALES of the PRINCES

CHAPTER ONE

The First Princes

"Rise! — they have risen; of brave Aneurin ask
How they have scourged old foes, perfidious friends,
The spirit of Caractacus descends
Upon the Patriots . . . "

William Wordsworth.

AT THE time of Llywelyn the Great, towards the end of the twelfth century, Wales was a land inhabited by semi-nomadic people who lived a simple, pastoral life. The rivers were full of salmon and trout and large colonies of beaver lived along the River Teifi. The only land suitable for agriculture was in Anglesey (Gwynedd), parts of Pembroke (Dyfed), and further south in Glamorgan.

There was no need to use money, and no Welsh ruler ever had a coin minted for him. Instead, the people were self-supporting and lived well on the produce of their herds of cattle and flocks of sheep, probably bartering for other commodities. There was no urban development as there had been in England. York, Lincoln, Exeter, Norwich and London were already thriving centres of trade, proud of their cathedrals, numerous parish churches and houses belonging to rich merchants. London in 1180 was a bustling port, where goods from many countries were bought and sold. In contrast, dwellings in Wales were simple, easily re-built, and the people had few belongings. Luxuries were unusual among these hardened tribes who would go up into the mountains for the summer months searching for rich pastures, returning to the valleys during the cold, harsh winters. There were small towns, often located on earlier Roman sites, grouped around religious houses or cathedrals, but they did not compare with the cathedral cities of England.

For entertainment they would sit and listen to poetry and music. They had a gift for "part-singing", only known in England among the people of Yorkshire. Evenings would be spent around the communal fire, listening to the bard who held a revered position in the community. Hospitality was generous, and no doubt visiting relatives would be offered a lavish feast followed by story-telling when the achievements of their fore-fathers, and the legendary feats of ancient times would be recounted and embellished. Gerald of Wales, writing in the last decades of the twelfth century, described the people as shrewd, musical, witty and bold. Both men and women cut their hair short, shaped round their ears and eyes, although the women wore flowing white veils, which were folded "like a crown". They took great care of their teeth and cleaned them often with twigs, polishing them with woollen cloths until they shone like ivory. Like their ancestors, the Britons, the men shaved large areas of their bodies, leaving only the upper lip untouched to display moustaches. They delighted in the sound of words, as did their English neighbours, and the Welsh particularly enjoyed playing with the language using ambiguous or alliterative words to add humour to their anecdotes. They were a tribal people, and loyalty to the clan was essential. As well as hunting for food, which required specialised skills, there was constant warfare between rival groups which developed qualities of endurance and daring. The Cymry, however, were one great group, a family with internal squabbles but a family ready to unite against outsiders.

There were many ruling princes. Below them all the "freeborn" were of one rank, divided into smaller kindred groups. These groups held the land of the "kindred". They were responsible for arranging marriages, law-enforcement, and the general well-being of each member of the family. Descent through the male-line only was recognised, with the inheritance going to the strongest claimant in many cases. Brother fought brother for the right to rule. One township, or *Tref,* would be grouped with others into a district, the *Cantref,* or hundred towns. Later, the cantref became a *Commote* or neighbourhood, smaller areas which were easier to adminster on the same lines as a *Shire* in England. These towns were very small, not like English towns with much larger populations.

Living in his roughly-constructed *Neuadd,* or Hall, surrounded by his large family and protected by armed retainers, the local prince ruled supreme. The cantref supplied all his needs, food, arms and loyal fighters when the need arose. The "royal" sons were sent to neighbouring princes for their education, a scheme which often resulted in bloodshed when the fostered princeling decided to fight the legitimate heir for control of the territory. This particular custom, and the ancient laws which governed succession, created instability and inevitable hostility between brothers and cousins when a ruler died. But the strongest survived, and the tribal chiefs developed into royal demi-kings. In North Wales, Gwynedd was ruled by Owain Gwynedd from Aberffraw in Anglesey. Powys was ruled by Gruffydd of Gwenwynwyn while South Wales, the lands of Deheubarth, was held firmly by the Lord Rhys. There were several other minor princelings who governed smaller areas such as parts of Denbigh, Flint (both now part of Clwyd) and Radnor (now part of Powys). They too received tribute from their peasant subjects, lived in great Halls and commanded respect within their territories.

Along the border with England, and encroaching into the Wales we know today, were the lands known as the Marches. After William the Conqueror invaded England in 1066, he rewarded his powerful followers, the Norman barons, by giving them large estates. The lands of Eastern and Southern Wales, and the border counties, were held by aristocratic Norman families whose methods were harsh and cruel. The most powerful of these Marcher Lords were the Bohuns, the Clares and the Briouzes. They controlled Brecon (Powys), Glamorgan (now three counties), and Usk (Gwent). Radnor and the area of Chirk* (Clwyd) was held by the Mortimers of Wigmore, while the lands around Newport (Casnewydd) were held by the Fitzmartins.

Like their Welsh counterparts, these Norman barons ruled little "kingdoms", and they lived far enough away from the King of England to escape interference or punishment. They often fought with their Welsh neighbours, claiming lands, stealing booty, and re-arranging boundaries to suit themselves. Unable to fight back, the Welsh people of those areas were forced to submit to English-Norman rule, which brought some advantages but which also destroyed the identity of the people. The Normans built daunting castles throughout the countryside, fortresses which had not been seen in Wales before. Safe in their intimidating strongholds, the Normans maintained order, grew richer, and imposed a new form of bondage on

*This was formerly part of Powys Fadog, the lands in the area of Chirk Castle.

the people who had fought off the Saxons to remain free when England had submitted to the invaders.

In 1194, a grandson of Owain Gwynedd, an earlier ruler of North Wales, called Llywelyn ab Iorwerth, began to show qualities of great leadership and military daring. He deposed his uncle, Dafydd, and prepared to challenge these Marcher Lords who persisted in attacking Wales and the Welsh people.

At first wily King John appeared to show favour to Llywelyn. He even gave his illegitimate daughter Joan to be his wife in 1206. In 1210 the King suddenly turned against the powerful Welsh leader, and in 1211 he invaded Wales and beat the people into submission. He built a castle at Llanfarian near Aberystwyth which aroused deep hatred among the inhabitants. During the following year, a league of Welsh Princes was formed, under Llywelyn's leadership. The castle at Aberystwyth was captured and the invaders were beaten. The men of North Wales would not tolerate Normans in their midst.

Llywelyn's strength increased. His forces over-ran Powys and South Wales; Cardigan (Aberteifi) and Carmarthen (Caerfyddin) were captured; Pembroke (Penfro) was isolated, where Anglo-Norman and Flemish settlers were at the mercy of the Welsh. All these conquered lands were divided among the princes, all of whom were content to acknowledge Llywelyn as their supreme leader. They paid homage to the ruler of Wales. Llywelyn reinforced his position by arranging suitable marriages for his children, allying them to the great families who ruled the Marches. His daughter Gladys the Dark was contracted to Reginald de Braose, or Briouze as it was commonly written. After Reginald's death, Gladys married Ralph Mortimer of Wigmore, a union which was to have an important bearing on history at a later date.

Llywelyn was a cautious and shrewd man, a sensible, deep-thinking and humane prince who was not concerned with the trappings of royalty. He was more than a mere figure-head surrounded by pomp and ceremony. The Peace of Worcester in 1218 recognised him as an important ruler, and he was granted the custody of the castles of Aberteifi, Caerfyddin (both Dyfed), Montgomery and Powis (both Powys). From 1218-1240 relations between England and Wales were peaceful. There were sporadic outbursts and clashes, but the new king, Henry III and Llywelyn were friendly. The Welshman's son, David, was recognised as heir to the throne of Gwynedd.

Llywelyn adopted the title of Lord of Snowdon, Prince of Aberffraw. His aim was to pass on this newly-united kingdom in its entirety, ignoring the old laws of gavelkind which meant equal division of a father's possessions between his sons. In England the laws of inheritance worked well, as Llywelyn had seen, and he had no wish to see his country divided as tradition demanded.

He ordered the compilation of new laws, revised versions of the laws of Hywel Dda, the Good, which had been revered by the Welsh since their introduction in the early tenth century.

In 1240, Llywelyn the Great died. During his life-time he had changed the old order. Feuding tribal groups had become one great tribe of the Cymry, loyal to one lord who ruled the Principality with a firm and just approach that set him apart from lesser men. Yet no ruler of Wales has ever successfully overcome the geographical barrier between North and South. During the reign of Edward I, the castle-builder, men of South Wales would fight the Welshmen of the North. Owen Glyn Dwr would face the same problem in the fifteenth century. The division was not only caused by mountain ranges and valleys, but by a confusion of loyalties as English influence spread throughout South Wales.

David did succeed his father, strongly opposed by his brother Gruffydd who felt that he had a claim to the title and lands, but he died after six years. Everything outside the boundary of Gwynedd was lost. Aberteifi went to the Earl of Pembroke; Powys, the huge stretch of land on the eastern flank of Wales, reverted to the Crown; and all the lesser princes were compelled to pay homage to King Henry III. David left no sons to inherit, and his brother Gruffydd had died in 1244 while trying to escape from the Tower of London after being held prisoner first by David, then by the King. After an inter-family struggle another Llywelyn emerged as leader. He was the son of David's brother, and was known as Llywelyn ap Gruffydd, or Llywelyn the Last. By 1257 he controlled once more the lands that had been united by his famous grandfather. In England, Henry III had his own problems, and after two abortive attempts to quell the Welsh he was forced to withdraw to guard his other walls. In 1258, Llywelyn was able to declare himself supreme ruler of Wales.

The uprisings in England were settled by 1267, and Henry

decided to acknowledge Llywelyn formally as the ruler of Wales by the Treaty of Montgomery. The Welsh Prince agreed to pay Henry an annual indemnity, and in return he was to rule all the lands from Snowdon in the west to the Dee on the eastern boundary, and to the Teifi and Brecon (Aberhonddu) in the south. This large area now would include Gwynedd, Clwyd, Powys and most of Dyfed. However this Llywelyn also had problems with the men of the South centred around Dinefwr, near Llandeilo, the castle which had been the focal point for inhabitants of the old kingdom of Deheubarth. He too had a succession problem, and faced hostility from his own brother who fled to England with many associates to enlist the help of the enemy sovereign.

When Henry died in 1272, a new threat appeared on the horizon. Perhaps more arrogant, and certainly less shrewd, than his grandfather, Llywelyn the Last failed to recognise the danger. There were storm-clouds gathering in the East.

Various events caused Llywelyn to withold the indemnity he had formerly paid to Henry. When the time came, the new king, Edward I, received nothing from his Welsh neighbour. Haughty Llywelyn also refused to pay homage to the English sovereign as his overlord, and ignored an invitation to the coronation ceremony. He felt that he was strong enough to defy the English throne. In 1276 war was declared, and open hostilities were resumed.

Edward I, King of England from 1272 until 1307, was a brilliant strategist. He recognised that Snowdonia itself must be treated as a natural fortress and promptly besieged the whole area. Supplies were cut off by a blockade along the northern coast. Llywelyn was forced to surrender, having misjudged the situation completely, with the loss of all his territories. The lands were divided, and placed under several "lordships", each one swearing allegiance to the crown. A lasting peace seemed to have descended on the troubled land. Llywelyn's power was restricted and he was allowed to govern part of Gwynedd in conjuction with his brother David. Edward was not concerned with revenge but with peace and order.

The King began to lay the foundation for a permanent occupation, which would dissuade the Welsh from any more thoughts of rebellion. Between 1278 and 1281 he ordered the construction of great fortresses at Rhuddlan, Flint, Aberystwyth and Builth Wells (Llanfair-ym-Muallt). Formerly, English attacks had begun at such places as Chester, Hereford. Worcester and Shrewsbury, which meant a long march into Wales itself. Now the English were to have permanent bases in the Principality, new and forbidding castles such as the Welsh of the North had never seen before. They had their own castles such as Dolbadarn near Llanberis; Dolwyddelan some five miles from Betws-y-coed; Dinas Emrys near Beddgelert; Castell-y-Bere at Abergynolwyn, Tywyn, which was the last to submit to Edward I, and numerous smaller fortifications, often on sites that had been chosen by earlier generations who had fought the Romans. Edward's castles were to incorporate all the knowledge and skill that Europe could provide.

The Welsh fought back, in a last attempt to rid their country of the invaders, only to be defeated. There were small-scale uprisings which were soon dealt with by the English soldiers and their Welsh allies. The main resistance movements were met by a determined Edward I. Llywelyn died in 1282 at Irfon Bridge near Cilmery (Cilmeri) four miles west of Llanfair-ym-Muallt, in 1287; Rhys ap Maredudd led an uprising in South Wales; and the last attempt occurred in 1295 when Madoc ap Maredudd led a brief, desperate revolt with the result that the Welsh were squashed. The site of Llywelyn's last battle is still remembered, and mourners pay tribute to his memory at a ceremony which invokes deep emotions in the hearts of modern patriots.

More castles were built at Caernarfon, Conwy and Harlech, with the completion of the chain at Beaumaris in 1295. Their construction occupied several years, as hundreds of labourers and artisans laboured to erect monuments which would outlast time. This imposing network of magnificent English bases controlled Wales. Cleverly designed, they could be guarded by small garrisons with minimum effort. Every possible weakness was eradicated; every situation anticipated.

Adjacent to each castle, small "free boroughs" were created, new settlements inhabited by loyal English merchants and their families, on the pattern of English castle towns. The local Welsh held their lands as tenants, guarded by the central castle, controlled by the resident English lord who enforced English laws. The Welsh had to submit. For many, life did not change too much, as they were allowed to retain lands which they had always held. In the new towns, commerce brought prosperity and new trade. Development around Edward's castles introduced urban life to a population accustomed to rural habits, and many prospered.

The Statute of Rhuddlan in 1284 had demanded allegiance from the Welsh. The old laws of Hywel Dda had been replaced by English laws. Lands had been divided on the English plan, as shires, which were governed by the King's Sheriffs and Justices. Gwynedd, the Snowdon Kingdom, became Anglesey, Caernarfonshire and Merionethshire until 1974* when they again became Gwynedd. In the north-east were the counties of Flint and Denbigh. South Wales, already firmly held by Norman families, was divided into Cardigan, Carmarthen and Pembroke (now Dyfed), Glamorgan (now West, Mid and South Glamorgan), Brecon, Radnor and Montgomery (now Powys) and Monmouth (now Gwent). Radnor and Montgomery completed the circle on the eastern border with England.

Along the Marches the ruling families were the Greys of Ruthin and Dyffryn Clwyd; the Warrens of Bromfield and Yale; the Mortimers who held Chirk, Maelienydd and Radnor; and the Fitzalans of Oswestry and Clun. In the South, the Bohuns held Aberhonddu and the mighty Clares ruled Glamorgan. Welsh people lived alongside the English in the new boroughs, accepting Edward as their King. When his son was born, reputedly at Caernarfon, and crowned Prince of Wales in 1301, there were not many who were prepared to say otherwise. It was easier to accept the situation with resignation, as peace brought prosperity, and Edward was a just man who exacted no revenge.

Edward I's strategy ensured that there would be no more uprisings in Wales. His castles controlled the districts, and his men controlled the castles. Scotland remained a thorn in his side, and his efforts were directed to the north as he attempted to unite Britain. The Welsh people subsided into a defeated and fatalistic life of peaceful co-existence. It was to be a hundred years before that simmering, resentful pot once again boiled over with the appearance of a new saviour, Owen Glyn Dwr.

*The Local Government Act 1972 made changes to many administrative areas which had effect from 1st April 1974. This resulted in the 13 counties of Wales being amalgamated to form eight new and larger counties. These new counties are shown in brackets.

CHAPTER TWO

The Kings of England

"This England never did, nor never shall,
Lie at the foot of a conqueror,
But when it first did help to wound itself.
Now these her princes are come home again,
Come the three corners of the world in arms,
And we shall shock them; nought shall make us rue,
If England to itself do rest but true."

William Shakespeare.
King John. Act V scene vii.

DURING those distant days of bitter feuds and family strife, with murder and intrigue an unavoidable part of aristocratic inheritance, it is essential to unravel the family history of those who became Kings of England. Each king faced dangerous enemies within his own household and he had to guard constantly against over-eager relatives who were planning and scheming to assume the sovereign's power. That sovereign wielded unbridled control. Just as Llywelyn the Great in Wales had realised the necessity for ensuring a firm line of succession, which failed, the English Plantagenets sought to maintain a firm hold on their throne. Ever since the confusing days of England in the Dark Ages, men had scrambled and clawed their way to the prize; sudden deaths, depositions and the claims of illegitimate heirs are strewn across the years. The crown went to the strongest, or the one with fewest enemies.

William, Duke of Normandy, was the illegitimate son of Robert the Devil. He decided to invade England to claim the throne from Harold, a brother-in-law of Edward the Confessor, who had been elected by the Witan in January 1066. William proved to be an efficient ruler whose decision to list all his possessions gave England the *Domesday Book,* a unique record of inestimable value. His eldest son, Robert, became Duke of Normandy; William Rufus, his second son, inherited the English crown, to be succeeded by his younger brother, Henry I in 1100. Further complications ensued when Henry I's son and heir was drowned, and the King was compelled to name his daughter Matilda as the heir. A nephew, Stephen, refused to accept the situation, and his claim was supported by the people of London with the result that Stephen ruled England until his death in 1154. By the Treaty of Wallingford, Matilda's son, Henry, took precedence over Stephen's son, and became the founder of the House of Plantagenet.

Henry II reigned from 1154 until 1189. As the heir died when he was thirteen, his brother succeeded, and became known as Richard I, the Lionheart. In storybooks, these were the years of gallant knights and tournaments when the high-born nobles lived by a strict code of honour. Their sons were taught jousting, archery, hunting and falconry, while the low-born serfs were obliged to work, and fight, at their lord's command. The Saxons still resented their Norman masters. It was barely a hundred years since Harold had been killed at Hastings and William the Conqueror had invaded England, bringing his Norman nobles to fill every important position in the land. These were the days of Robin Hood and Ivanhoe, heroes of the down-trodden Saxons.

King Richard himself spoke a foreign language, Norman French. During the ten years of his reign he spent only a few months in England. He spent his time abroad, fighting expensive wars on the Continent and in the Holy Land. His bride, Berengaria, the daughter of the King of Navarre, never set foot in England. Richard was a prisoner in Germany for two years while his brother John ruled as regent, that evil brother who declined to ransom Richard, preferring his life as king while the true King rotted. As Richard left no immediate heir, John did become king in 1199. Subsequent actions reveal that he was a cruel and greedy monarch, and a dangerous ally, as Llywelyn discovered. His high-handed behaviour led to an unprecedented step which gave England an institution we now prize very highly. His barons compelled him to sign, or affix his seal, to Magna Carta, to safe-guard their own interests at the time, but which provided a foundation for the legal rights of everyone today.

John was succeeded by Henry III, the young king who was more friendly towards Llywelyn, and more trustworthy. Henry allowed the Welshman to be known as the Prince of Aberffraw, accepting David as the heir to the Welsh throne. Acceptance of this kingdom on his doorstep is not unusual if Wales is placed in the context of Europe at this time. There were many small kingdoms within France, or Spain, or neighbouring countries, which claimed a separate identity and independence. The thrones of these tiny, often rich, realms were the cause of many battles. Tactical marriages between sovereigns and their heirs complicated matters even further, and it was these hereditary claims which involved England and France in the wars which ended during the fifteenth century. Llywelyn had every reason to believe that his Wales would continue as a kingdom, as it compared in size if not in wealth, with many others.

In England, Henry tried to abrogate the precious Charter as the new laws hampered his power. The monarch no longer wielded absolute power as earlier rulers had done. He had to face a rebellion led by Simon de Montfort, assisted by many Norman barons, which resulted in the confinement of the King and his son. Before his release, the foundations for a Parliament were laid, and accepted. England had achieved a formal and elected government which would curb the King's excesses, hopefully to prevent the abuse of the sovereign's privileged position such as they had suffered at the hands of King John. Simon de Montfort's Westminster Parliament of January, 1265 marked the beginning of Representation. In addition to the clergy and the barons, who would have been expected to attend, every shire was invited to send two knights, and every borough two burgesses. Instead of deposing the King, which would not have been difficult, Simon de Montfort introduced a system which gave England some stability. It was not perfect, and was to be abused several times in the centuries which followed, but Parliament was established to shackle the monarch and to protect the citizens. By this time, the English had grown accustomed to paying taxes. England had a fair legal system which was enforced throughout the country. The people had also grown accustomed to fighting for their respective landlords, the knights who were responsible for providing soldiers in whatever wars arose. William I had united England for the first time, and while England developed along a steady path, merging into one nation as Saxons and Normans forgot their animosity, Wales remained fragmented.

Edward I succeeded in 1272, and went on to conquer the rebels of Wales, forcing them to follow the English road and to obey English laws. His great castles remain today to remind us of his strength and military genius. Without leaders, the Welsh lived their hard lives alongside English neighbours, absorbing Saxon-Norman ideas which were not all unwelcome. Events in England swept on towards great changes.

1307 saw Edward II on the throne. He reigned until 1327 when he was deposed and murdered. A weak and effeminate man, so unlike his soldier father, Edward led his men to the disastrous defeat at Bannockburn, where they were massacred by Robert the Bruce and his fierce Scots. He was easily swayed by flatterers. First one family tried to gain power over him, then another. Even his wife, a French princess, was his enemy and she was forced to leave her husband to the tender mercies of his favourite courtier, Hugh Despenser. Civil war tore England apart as men such as Thomas of Lancaster and Roger Mortimer, the Earl of March, fought against the King's friends, and between themselves. Queen Isabella was sent to France in 1325, where she formed an alliance with Mortimer, who had escaped from the Tower in 1323. The heir, Prince Edward, joined them across the Channel to do homage to King Charles in place of his father who had been defeated in a war in Gascony. In 1326, they returned with an army, and were joined by other magnates who were disillusioned with their temperamental monarch. Edward finally met his death under mysterious circumstances at Berkeley Castle in Gloucestershire. His supporters were defeated, and his friends were executed. Before his murder a deed of resignation in favour of his eldest son had been forced from him at Kenilworth.

Edward III, and his children, bring us to an important division in the line of succession. He reigned from 1327 until 1377, fifty years of stable rule which lasted long enough to supply the royal house of later years with new claimants. At his accession, the King was a minor, and England was governed by a regency council which almost resulted in disaster. Edward was more like his grandfather than his father, and quickly asserted himself to take the initiative in 1330, to rule and not be ruled.

However, where Edward I had essentially sought peace, Edward III was a warrior, and his friends were soldiers or the sons of soldiers. He claimed the French throne through his mother, Isabella, and intent on glory, the King planned an invasion through the Low Countries. To assist his plans, he married Philippa, the daughter of the Count of Hainault. In 1346, the King crossed over to Normandy with a huge army and marched unhindered through the country which had once sent an army into England. On 26th August, the English met the French at Crecy, where infantry and archers proved their supremacy by slaughtering the French cavalry. Edward's first son, also Edward, was known as the Black Prince because of his armour which was of dark steel. This Prince of Wales took his crest, three feathers and the motto "Ich Dien", I serve, from the defeated King of Bohemia after Crecy. The Prince won yet more fame at Poitiers and was the idol of the English people. He had married Joan, the Fair Maid of Kent, whose father Edmund was also a son of Edward I. It was their son, Richard of Bordeaux, who was to succeed Edward III in 1377 as Richard II. The Black Prince unfortunately died before his father, while on a campaign near Bordeaux.

Richard II was the last of these Plantagenet kings, rulers whose claims to the throne were hereditary and unchallenged, since there was no argument or dispute to cloud the issue of their legitimate succession. While some of their actions and decisions caused dissension, their right to rule could not be questioned. Great pomp and splendour accompanied the royal personage and his court. For the rich and powerful, this medieval England was a kingdom of fair ladies and powerful, brave knights; of tournaments and gaily-decked chargers; of noble thoughts and noble deeds. People recognised the sanctity of the throne, with the King as God's chosen representative on earth, chosen by Divine Right. If he were cruel and greedy, ill or insane, then that was unfortunate; his person was still sacrosanct. The lives of ordinary people were miserable and uncertain. Diseases, such as the plague, were part of everyday life. After years of war with France, when men had been forced to leave their homes to fight while those left behind starved, the extravagance of King Richard and his courtiers drove some to rebellion. Yet the reverence felt by people for their monarch, and the belief in the Divine Right, enabled Richard to remain on his throne, leading a life of luxury and excess. Taxation had become an unavoidable irritant, but people paid their taxes from their meagre incomes without too much argument. They grumbled privately but open rebellion was rare. Social changes were taking place slowly, and men discovered that their services were valuable. Many serfs, former bond-servants, achieved freedom by agreement with their masters; some simply absconded, and sought work for better wages under a new master. There was talk of "Equality", encouraged by men such as John Ball; there were heretical theories which suggested that men should withold their services and rents if their masters were not worthy. Lack of political power meant that such subversion could not be effective, and the brief Peasants' Revolt was quickly quelled by the personal appearance of young King Richard.

It was at this time during Richard's reign that Owen Glyn Dwr was growing up. The sons of the nobility were well-educated, trained in the heraldic arts, taught to joust, to sit a horse and to wield a lance. Boys were sent to the new universities at Oxford and Cambridge, or to the Inns of the Court. They were expected to serve as squires in the households of the nobility, which enabled them to travel and learn the customs of England's aristocracy. The wars with France gave them an opportunity to observe the customs of foreign nobles, and the rules of chivalric warfare which flourished alongside the carnage of medieval battles. They accompanied their protectors, who travelled with enormous entourages, learning how to conduct themselves as knights and well-born gentlemen. The art of dressing for battle in complicated suits of armour; the methods of using the variety of weapons; the skills, horsemanship and conduct of established knights often were an example to these eager young boys whose dreams centred around military prowess. That death could be inglorious was a possibility that did not tarnish the vision. Illustrious knights often suffocated in their armour, unable to rise from the ground after being unseated. Thousands died of unpleasant diseases such as dysentery, which swept through the camps attacking nobles and peasants alike. But victory brought rich rewards, ransoms and, the gratitude of a grateful monarch, new titles. Edward III had introduced the Order of the Garter, in 1348, bestowing a mystical reverence on those knights who achieved most glory. Boys were sent away from home when they were very young, nine or ten years old, exchanged among relatives and noble neighbours, often spending many years away from their own families. They learned by example, and there was no room for the interfering love and affection that might have been shown by mothers.

There were few opportunities in Richard's reign for ambitious soldiers to win a glorious reputation. Edward's wars had left both France and England in a very weakened condition. The King's marriages to Anne of Bohemia and later to Isabella, daughter of Charles VI of France, bought a temporary truce, and life at court took precedence. Nobles were reduced to fighting amongst themselves as they looked for power within the kingdom, as jealousies and intrigue made life precarious for those nearest to the King.

Dark forces were to end the years of chivalry and lavish living. A conspiracy of great nobles, under the banner of Henry of Lancaster, captured Richard at Flint Castle and forced him to abdicate before he was imprisoned at Pontefract where he was probably either starved or stabbed to death. This Henry became Henry IV, and he was the first king to assume the title and then ask Parliament for confirmation of his position. He had broken the chain of hereditary title. When he committed this great sin in 1399, he could not have envisaged the wearisome years ahead. During his uneasy reign of fourteen years he faced hostility from his own subjects, wars with Ireland and Scotland, possible war with France, and a rebellion from the west when Owen Glyn Dwr led the Welsh against the royal army. Many of the lower classes refused to believe that Richard was dead, and the usurper was not popular with the loyalists of Cheshire and regions on the Welsh border. They were convinced that the royal prisoner lived, and that he could be freed to lead them against the Bolingbroke traitor. Later those beliefs were to help Glyn Dwr. Throughout Henry's reign, the longheld belief that a King's person was inviolate was to plague the man who had the temerity to murder God's anointed. The enormity of the crime guaranteed Henry a place in hell.

Henry's claim to the throne was as a cousin of Richard II. Edward III had several children, which led to disruption of the royal line. His eldest son, the Black Prince, died in 1376 while on a campaign leaving Richard, the grandson, to inherit the throne. Edward's second son had also died. The third son was Lionel, Duke of Clarence, who married Elizabeth of Ulster. This marriage was to become important many years later since their daughter, Philippa, married Edmund Mortimer, the great Earl of March. The son of that union was Roger Mortimer, who was therefore the legitimate heir to the throne through the female line if Richard provided no heirs himself, a distinct possibility when it was common knowledge that the King preferred his courtiers to his wives. This line eventually formed the House of York.

The fourth son, John of Gaunt, who lived much of his early life in the shadow of his celebrated brother Edward, became the mighty Duke of Lancaster. He had become undisputed leader of the magnates who ruled England during Richard's minority, and the son of his first marriage to the beautiful Blanche of Lancaster, was Henry, the third grandson. In order of seniority Henry, born at Bolingbroke Castle, came a long way down the list of hopefuls.

Henry became the first king of the House of Lancaster after deposing his cousin, and set a precedent for later claimants. He had married Mary, the daughter of Humphrey de Bohun, Earl of Hereford. 'Their son was also called Henry, the Prince Hal of Shakespeare who became Henry V. Both Henry IV and his son were to be involved in the career of Owen Glyn Dwr.

They were times of great change and upheaval, in Wales, Scotland and Ireland. The English throne was threatened from every side, and from within. Those same nobles who had put Henry on to the throne would try to put him off again. The people were unsure; some were glad that the "extravagant King" was dead; others feared worse at the hands of the new King, the stern and cold-natured Bolingbroke. His greatest contribution to the medieval way of life was unintentional, as he demonstrated that kings were not protected by God and that they were mortals who could be eliminated.

The great social changes, which had begun slowly after the plagues of the fourteenth century, were to continue in the new climate. Parliament was to increase its power, and Henry discovered that a King could no longer govern autocratically. Seeing his example, others decided that men could seize power by force as they had done in the Dark Ages. The usurper's legacy, after the short and glorious reign of his son, was turmoil, as the Wars of the Roses destroyed what was left of medieval England.

Although Henry won the prize, he almost lost the contest.

"The woe's to come; the children yet unborn
Shall feel this day as sharp to them as thorn"

Richard II, Act IV scene i

CHAPTER THREE

Victim and Victor . . . Richard and Henry

"Tell Bolingbroke, — for yond methinks he is, —
That every stride he makes upon my land
Is dangerous treason; he is come to ope
The purple testament of bleeding war;
But ere the crown he looks for live in peace,
Ten thousand bloody crowns of mothers' sons
Shall ill become the flower of England's face . . . "

William Shakespeare.
King Richard II Act III scene iii

IT IS important to understand something of the characters who were involved in this episode of English history, since they were known personally to Owen Glyn Dwr. Events in England, and the subsequent conflict between powerful factions, were to involve Wales in a bitter struggle.

Shakespeare portrayed Richard II as a weak, arrogant, selfish man, in direct contrast to the ambitious Henry, surnamed Bolingbroke, Duke of Hereford, whose actions appear almost mechanical and without emotion. Poor self-pitying Richard is provided with poetry as he bewails his mis-fortunes, his only strength the allegiance of one or two true friends and the dubious fidelity of shallow sycophants. The warrior politician Henry quickly despatches the snivelling monarch to Pontefract and oblivion. Richard's death brought an end to medieval pageantry, personified by the King ruling his "scepter'd isle", to be replaced by the sterner rule of Lancaster.

Henry did not achieve the throne alone. There were rapacious lords ready to assist him, notably the Earl of Northumberland and his son. This rich northern family, the House of Percy, could raise loyal military support at a moment's notice as they lived in the marches of Northern England which faced perennial attacks from the Scots. Henry Percy was an exceptional and wily commander. His son, known as Hotspur, had been brought up in the same tradition, respected and feared for his prowess. These two, together with the Earl's brother Thomas, Earl of Worcester, were wealthy landowners in control of their own private armies, and they did not hesitate to assume the role of kingmakers when the opportunity came. In the play *Richard II,* the King says, "Northumberland, thou ladder wherewithal The mounting Bolingbroke ascends my throne . . ." (Act V scene i) adding that the future may reveal new ambitions to the man who has already disposed of one king and created another. Capable of insincerity and almost obsequious behaviour when the occasion demanded, the Earl emerges as an untrustworthy ally. Accompanying Henry on his march across England, Northumberland declares that it would have been a weary journey without the beguiling company of his friend. From the beginning he is a man whose allegiance shifts from one side to the other.

When Shakespeare wrote these history plays, almost two hundred years after the events, he had to rely on the chronicles of earlier times which were not always accurate, or without prejudice. He refers to specific events which took place, but the time sequence often differed from the truth. The characterisations are the result of his own genius. By piecing together historical items of information, hearsay, legend and folk-lore, the men of those times come to life complete with their vices, virtues, honour and dishonour. The Lancaster rebellion was the result of Richard's egoism and greed.

Henry, born at Bolingbroke Castle in Lincolnshire, was the eldest son of John of Gaunt, the Duke of Lancaster, fourth son of Edward III. As a direct descendant of this revered English monarch, Henry, Earl of Derby and Duke of Hereford, was second in succession to the throne after his cousin Edmund Mortimer, Earl of March, son of Edward III's third son, the Duke of Clarence. At the age of nineteen, John of Gaunt married his cousin Blanche and acquired half the estates of the House of Lancaster. When Blanche's sister died soon afterwards, all the estates came under his control with the result that he became one of the most rich and powerful men in England, equalling the wealth and power of Richard himself. The Lancaster inheritance included some thirty castles in strategic positions throughout the kingdom. In 1385 John of Gaunt was able to put 1,000 men-at-arms and 3,000 archers at Richard's disposal during the Scottish expedition of that year.

In 1387 there was an attempt to overthrow those favourites of King Richard who were proving dangerous to many of the wealthy lords and landowners who had to pay for the court's extravagances. At the Battle of Radcot Bridge, (1387), these Lords Appellant successfully destroyed those who threatened their security. The leaders, the Earls of Arundel, Warwick and Nottingham, the Duke of Gloucester and Henry Bolingbroke were to escape Richard's punishment at the time, but ten years afterwards the King was in a stronger position and took his revenge. In 1398 Gloucester was murdered; the Earl of Arundel was executed while his brother Thomas, Archbishop of Canterbury and the Earl of Warwick were banished. Bolingbroke and Mowbray, the Duke of Norfolk, were apparently forgiven, but Richard was a treacherous master who had lost some of his dearest friends at Radcot Bridge, on the Thames in Oxfordshire.

Mowbray suspected the King's motives, and certain confidential but treasonable remarks were relayed to the King by Bolingbroke on his father's advice. It is at this point that the play begins, when Richard has called both men, "the accuser and the accused" to explain. A grand tournament was arranged at Coventry, and men travelled from far and wide to attend the spectacle.

It was to have been a fight to the death in true chivalric tradition; but the crowd was cheated. For some reason Richard chose to banish both men rather than allow a combat to prove their loyalty. Mowbray was exiled for life; Henry, Duke of Hereford was banished for ten years — even though his father was the King's most powerful noble and ally. The old Duke of Lancaster must have found the decision hard to bear, but he accepted his sovereign's judgement without argument.

In February 1399 John of Gaunt died. For Richard it was a fortuitous demise. He promptly confiscated all the wealth and lands of the House of Lancaster, the inheritance of Henry Bolingbroke, the new Earl of Lancaster, and the absent heir was banished for life. The King must have felt extremely secure, but this action on the death of his most respected supporter provoked much sympathy for Henry, exiled and disinherited by a scheming, spendthrift king. It was inevitable that many of the other great landowners should speculate on the possibility that their own estates would follow Lancaster's if the King felt so inclined. Richard needed money to finance an expedition to Ireland where he hoped to restore peace and gain a reputation.

Apparently unaware of the reactions he may have aroused, or shielded from such speculations by his circle of flattering friends, the King gathered an army and set off across the Irish Sea, leaving the throne virtually unguarded. Among his retinue was Bolingbroke's son, Henry of Monmouth, who was twelve years old. The Keeper of the Realm, left behind to manage England's affairs, was Edmund of Langley, the ineffectual Duke of York.

From Boulogne, Henry sailed to Ravenspur on the Humber in Yorkshire. He marched unchallenged across the country to Bristol, attracting supporters as he made his triumphant progress from Lancaster-owned castle to castle. Edmund was not a military commander; he was unable, or unwilling, to offer any resistance. Richard's lesser captains were not prepared to fight the troops of Bolingbroke and his allies, the Percies and Nevilles, who presented an intimidating, united front. The King's small army in Wales lacked leadership and the men who had been Richard's most loyal soldiers, the Cheshire archers, stripped off their white hart badges and slunk away.

The royal forces were further divided for the crossing from Ireland, a blunder which left only a tiny faction to protect the King on his journey to Conwy Castle. His closest friends were captured and executed; another defected. Even his faithful old dog was attracted to the enemy.

Shakespeare's Bolingbroke insists that he seeks only the inheritance that is legally his, not the crown of England. Richard, at Henry's mercy, cannot believe that a Lancaster would stop short when there was a kingdom to be taken, an unprotected, glittering crown to be snatched. After his capitulation at Flint Castle, Richard is taken to London where he abdicates of his own free will.

It seems likely that Richard was murdered on Henry's orders as the deposed King was a constant threat. Bolingbroke must have learned from his predecessor's mistakes and did not allow a possibly dangerous enemy to live. Shakespeare is kinder, giving Henry the benefit of the doubt:

> "... *though I did wish him dead*
> *I hate the murderer, loved him murdered.*"

Act V scene v.

(i) The double-towered gatehouse of Rhuddlan Castle.

(ii) Countryside surrounding Rhuddlan Castle.

(iii) Dolwyddelan Castle near Betws y Coed. *Robert Haworth*

(iv) The River Dee at Carrog.

(v) Flint Castle.

(vi) The grassy mound of Sycharth near Llansilin.

(vii) Owen Glyn Dwr's Mount visible from the main road near Carrog.

(viii) Cymmer Abbey near Dolgellau. *Robert Haworth*

(ix) Looking towards Hyddgen from the Nant y Moch Reservoir.

(x) The Great Hall at Conwy Castle.

(xi) Llanbadarn Castle, Aberystwyth.

(xii) Caernarfon Castle.

Robert Haworth

On 13th October, 1399, Henry, Duke of Hereford and Lancaster, was crowned King Henry IV of England. His eldest son, Henry of Monmouth, was brought from Trim in Ireland to carry the sword of justice at the coronation. That November the young man was invested with the titles Prince of Wales, Duke of Cornwall and Earl of Chester.

The sanctity of the throne is stressed throughout *Richard II,* while Bolingbroke the usurper is condemned. The play ends with Henry planning a voyage to the Holy Land where he hopes to atone for his dreadful crime against God. *Henry IV, Part One,* opens with this same theme as the King outlines his plan for a Holy War, but the wars within Britain prevent his excursion. At the conclusion of *Henry IV, Part Two,* the King is still suffering from guilt, talking of a crusade to save his soul from everlasting perdition. He tells his son,

> " . . . *God knows, my son,*
> *By what by-paths and indirect crook'd ways*
> *I met this crown . . .* "

Act IV scene iv

These two Kings, the one pleasure-loving and sensitive to all that was beautiful, the other an unimaginative soldier, were to blame for the events which tore England and Wales apart.

While the earliest historians depicted Owen Glyn Dwr as a savage, uncouth Welsh rebel leading roving bands of vicious thugs on forays against the peaceable English, Shakespeare painted a different picture, from undiscovered sources. The undisputed facts about Richard II's reign, which give some insight into the King's character, were available in Holinshed, Froissart and other contemporary chronicles, annals and records. Information about the Welshman was more difficult to acquire, as the English had never professed any great interest in what happened among the tribe over the border. Thomas Phaer in the *Mirror for Magistrates* had encouraged the English to view their neighbours as they had always done. The ambitious Welshman had met a miserable end as a result of his schemes, a suitable end for a scoundrel.

The Owen Glendower of *Henry IV, Part One,* written in 1597-8, is closer to Glyn Dwr's character than any of the later, prejudiced descriptions in the accounts of historians right up to the eighteenth century. There is evidence that Shakespeare had Welsh-born friends, and that he had a knowledge of Welsh history which may have inspired his own more sympathetic treatment of the "traitor".

Owen was no heathen barbarian, descending like a wolf from his cave in the hills to attack the innocent English. He was a highly-educated, accomplished, noble man of considerable talents, who lived in a beautiful home surrounded by a loving family.

Shakespeare's first reference to Glendower follows the popular belief, perhaps to make the audience of his day feel more comfortable with a character they would know as a savage foreigner.

As Henry contemplates his situation, with England at peace, the Earl of Westmoreland destroys his hopes with the news:

" . . . there came
A post from Wales loaden with heavy news;
Whose worst was, that the noble Mortimer
Leading the men of Herefordshire to fight
Against the irregular and wild Glendower,
Was by the hands of that rude Welshman taken,
A thousand of his people butchered . . . "

Act I scene i.

Yet, as the play develops, Glendower is revealed as a man who is susceptible to music and poetry, a cultured and clever strategist respected by the great House of Northumberland and treated as their equal. He tells Mortimer, his son-in-law,

"She bids you on the wanton rushes lay you down,
And rest your gentle head upon her lap,
And she will sing the song that pleaseth you
And on your eye-lids crown the god of sleep,
Charming your blood . . . "

Act III scene i

"She" is his daughter, the Welsh-speaking Lady Mortimer who must speak to her husband with her eyes since she cannot converse in English. Her ability to sing sweet songs reflects the national talent of the Welsh people, a talent that must have been recognised in Elizabethan times. This domestic scene of love and gentleness is a pretty interlude in the middle of turmoil and strife.

The young Prince Hal, Prince of Wales, is contrasted strongly with Hotspur, the fiery son of the Earl of Northumberland. Historically there was quite an age difference, but here they are presented as dashing young men, the chivalrous grace of the Prince emerging clearly against the rough Northern manners of Hotspur. Even in those days anyone living north of the Midlands was probably regarded as a boor by the sophisticated Londoners.

This Cock of the North demonstrates the early practicality of the Englishman, directly contrasted with the Welsh magician whose magnetism affected his own countrymen so dramatically and who instilled such patriotism. Glyn Dwr and Hotspur were friends, and later allies during the rebellion. Some of this familiarity is revealed in the play as Hotspur makes fun of Owen's seriousness and his belief in omens. The Welshman's reply to the teasing,

> " . . . *Cousin, of many men*
> *I do not bear these crossings. Give me leave*
> *To tell you once again that at my birth*
> *The front of heaven was full of fiery shapes,*
> *The goats ran from the mountains, and the herds,*
> *Were strangely clamorous to the frighted fields.*"

Act III scene i

Hotspur is unimpressed by this superstitious nonsense, and their argument continues:

Glendower: "I can call spirits from the vasty deep."

Hotspur: "Why, so can I; or so can any man; But will they come when you do call for them?"

This is however a minor altercation and they obviously respected each other as soldiers. Mortimer remarks:

> "*In faith, he is a worthy gentleman,*
> *Exceedingly well read, and profited*
> *In strange concealments, valiant as a lion*
> *And wondrous affable and as bountiful*
> *As mines in India. Shall I tell you, cousin?*

He holds your temper in a high respect
And curbs himself even of his natural scope
When you do cross his humour: faith he does . . . "

Act III scene i

This is the man who was to lead the Welsh against the might of England's army, as "valiant as a lion", and as dangerous to Henry Bolingbroke as any of the enemies both within and without his kingdom's boundaries.

Shakespeare's Glendower reminds Hotspur,

"I can speak English, lord, as well as you;
For I was train'd up in the English court;
Where, being but young, I framed to the harp
Many an English ditty lovely well."

Act III scene i

As the son of a wealthy family Glyn Dwr had, indeed, received a thorough education in England during the reign of Richard II, the King that "every day under his household roof did keep ten thousand men."

Placed as he is, alongside these two experienced veterans, it is difficult to remember that Prince Henry was a boy and not a man at the outbreak of hostilities. Shakespeare's portrait of Hal was in preparation for his emergence as Henry V, consequently his carefree boyhood was exaggerated to emphasise the emergence of the hero of Agincourt in his later play.

That he was a born soldier cannot be disputed, as harsh training from the cradle had ensured that he could not be otherwise. He had military guardians, such as Hotspur, to instruct him while his father was occupied with affairs of state. He would not have known his father well, but that was not unusual for a young boy of his class in the fourteenth century. From his birth in 1387 young Henry of Monmouth was reared in the family tradition inspired by his grandfather, John of Gaunt and great-grandfather, Edward III. The boy would have been constantly on the move from castle to castle, learning geography as an indirect result of his travels, and history from those servants and retainers who had played an active part in events as they had happened. Crecy and Poitiers were recent victories to them.

While his education would not have been strictly formal, he did learn to read and write, and to appreciate music. He enjoyed himself hunting and took part in tournaments, showing an early talent and delight in such knightly pastimes. As the grandson of John of Gaunt he would have inherited countless loyal servants, and soldiers, and although his father was in exile he accompanied the doomed King Richard to Ireland as a squire, to learn the art of warfare. The twelve year-old boy had seen many proud men come and go.

Shakespeare's Prince Hal is a tavern-loving youth who kept disreputable company. Yet his intelligence and chivalry are shown quite clearly, qualities which develop as he matures before graduating as the glorious Henry V. The real Prince had these qualities.

This youth was Glendower's opponent, in the play and in reality.

This illustrious son of England was entrusted with the task of subduing the Welsh dragon, of driving him from his lair to quell insurrection once and for all.

These then are the principal actors in the story of Owen Glyn Dwr. Richard is deposed by Henry, and the subsequent actions of Henry Bolingbroke, Prince Henry, together with Northumberland and his son Hotspur lead to the Welsh rebellion of 1400. The historical background and the characters of the people involved may help to explain the brief, and unsuccessful attempt of this well-educated and Anglicised Welshman to free his country from the grip of the House of Lancaster. New loyalties and new alliances changed the pattern of an established system as England was torn apart and Wales fought for freedom. Shakespeare's characterisations enable us to see the participants as vulnerable people, men with admirable strengths but with very human weaknesses. The soil of Henry's kingdom was to be soaked in the blood of "her own children."

CHAPTER FOUR

Growing Up

"A Knight ther was, and that a worthy man
That fro the tyme that he first bigan
To ryden out, he loved chivalrye,
Trouthe and honour, fredom and curteisye."

Geoffrey Chaucer.
The Canterbury Tales

ALTHOUGH Shakespeare's Glendower maintained that at his birth there were strange portents and great omens, there is no definite date to be found for the birthday of Owen Glyn Dwr. It remains a mystery. This preoccupation with supernatural phenomena was accepted by rational Englishmen as part of the Welsh character, and treated with an amused tolerance, or contempt. Throughout the *Anglo-Saxon Chronicle* there are references to unusual occurrences in the heavens ranging from solar and lunar eclipses to wonderful comets and inexplicable lights. Such happenings were regarded with some awe, and it is easy to understand the terror of superstitious peasants and their more educated masters when the moon turned blue or a huge comet lit the daytime sky.

The more urbane Englishmen of Elizabethan times regarded the beliefs of their more primitive Welsh neighbours with wry amusement. While they themselves could offer no rational or scientific explanations they obviously considered themselves to be intelligent enough to disregard such portents and ill-omens. They were, after all, protected by God. Richard II's Welsh captain used such strange events as an excuse to abandon the field. He knew that they foretold the "death or fall of Kings", (Act II scene iv). The religious folk of England knew that the pagans over the border were still living in the days of Druids and magicians.

Since historical records at the time were not compiled with an eye for accuracy, it is not surprising that the birth, or death, of any notorious man would later be embellished with tales of glowing fireballs or the appearance of blood in unlikely places.

Legend and folk-memory have supplied a date of 1349, a year of pestilence and plague for Glyn Dwr's birth, the reign of the Black Death. Pennant's account of the life of Glyn Dwr quotes 1354, apparently gleaned from an old manuscript. As the same source gives information that Owen died at the age of forty-six, the year of his death would have been 1400 which means that Pennant's source must be wrong. The assertion that the hero's birth coincided with a year of disaster, when the population of Britain was decimated by disease, may also be the conjecture of later chroniclers who regarded the Welshman as a scourge.

Definite evidence is supplied by the account of a long and tedious trial, during which Glyn Dwr was certainly a witness. These manuscripts record his age at the time of the trial as twenty-seven, or thereabouts, providing a year of birth, 1359. Thus at the beginning of the rebellion he would have been in his prime, and not an old soldier of fifty-one, or a dead man. There were however discrepancies even in this convincing record as it was common practice to enter someone's age at twenty-seven years "et pluis", rather as we use "over twenty-one". Another witness, Geoffrey Chaucer, is described as forty "et pluis" when he was almost certainly fifty-eight. While such errors may have been complimentary to the witnesses they are confusing to historians. It is not likely that a clerk's assessment of the age of a young man would produce such a large discrepancy so it does seem likely that the Lord of Glendore* was no more than thirty years old.

This confusion may be untangled further if yet more evidence is introduced. There was a secondary plague in 1361 which claimed many more victims and added to the misery of the defenceless populace. At the beginning of 1362 there were terrible storms and in March 1362 a comet lit the skies for approximately four weeks. The plague and the storm are referred to by William Langland in *The Vision of Piers Plowman* and the comet was recorded by Chinese observers who had already begun to take a scientific interest in these visitors from space. These memorable events, so close to the probable year of Glyn Dwr's birth, may explain both the dimly-recalled "truth" of legend and the more usual and acceptable truth of the Chester trial.

*Glendore was the clerk's spelling of an unwieldy Welsh name in the records of the trial: his brother was described as Tuder de Glyndore.

His place of birth also remains undiscovered. The family estates were centred at Carrog in Gwynedd, and at Sycharth on the other side of the Berwyn Mountains near Oswestry.

The lordships of Glyndyfrdwy and Ial had been held by Owen's family since 1270 when Gruffudd Fychan inherited this portion of Northern Powys from his father, Gruffudd ap Madog, Prince of Powys Fadog. After the Welsh revolt of 1282, Ial, or Yale, became the property of the Earl of Surrey, but Gruffudd Fychan managed to retain Glyndyfrdwy. By the year 1300, the estates of Cynllaith Owain — the site of Sycharth — were also part of the family inheritance. It would seem likely that he was born at one or the other of these ancestral homes, but some sources insist that he was born at Trefgarn Owain near St David's (Tyddewi) in Pembrokeshire. That particular property belonged to his aunt, not to his mother, yet he could have been born in the South. Owen's mother, Helen, was the daughter of Llywelyn ap Rhys of Penfro and Aberteifi. It was this connection with the royal house of Deheubarth in South Wales that was to prove invaluable in his later life. Helen's sister Margaret was married to William of Mawddwy, and it was to her that the estates at Trefgarn Owain had passed on the death of their father. The argument and speculation do not alter the story. Lloyd George, the Welsh Wizard of this century, was born in Manchester, but his allegiance and nationality were never affected by such a minor accident.

It seems certain that Glyn Dwr was sent to Westminster in his early youth, to study law, and to improve his education generally since legal training then was similar to a university course today. Actual records of the Inns of Court began in 1422, so the supposition cannot be proved by written evidence. Glyn Dwr's knowledge of legal matters is, however, indisputable. It was there at Westminster that he acquired polish, good manners and the ability to mix freely with other sons of the nobility.

He would have been taught heraldic history and all the gentlemanly accomplishments of a chivalric age, basic requirements in the age of Richard II. University entrance in those days was for boys of ten or eleven upwards. Later they would be schooled in military matters and were often hardened soldiers while still in their teens. Perhaps Glyn Dwr attended one of the established universities of Oxford or Cambridge for a short time as there were many Welsh-born students enjoying their freedom at these English institutions. Some of these young fire-brands were to join him years later when England was not so friendly towards the foreigners from Wales. Students of the twentieth century are often the first to publicise a cause, and the young men of Oxford in 1400 were quick to promote unrest and to cause disturbances in the streets with their drinking and fighting.

From scholastic studies, Glyn Dwr moved on, to become a squire in the household of some noble where he learned the art of the soldier. Possibly he was in the service of Henry Bolingbroke, the King's cousin, and he would also have encountered many other important lords both at Richard's court and on military campaigns. Glyn Dwr's family were neighbours of the Earl of Arundel so it is possible that he acted as squire to the Earl and not to Bolingbroke as some accounts suggest. As Glyn Dwr was to become a baron in his own right it may be misleading to describe him as a "squire". When called upon to fight in the King's name, all the knights of a particular area were responsible for organizing the necessary forces under the leadership of an over-lord acting as a general. These squires, knights and barons would be instructed to bring soldiers to join the main force. Youths who were in service to more experienced lords were able to learn the complicated art of warfare by assisting and observing. Dressing a knight for battle, or for a tournament, was a complicated procedure. The sons of the wealthy were expected to act in this capacity until they were taught horsemanship and weaponry which would enable them to fight in their own battles. Thus the squires gained valuable knowledge and, eventually, employed squires of their own.

From the time of Edward I the lords and barons of the Welsh Marches, the lands spreadeagled across the modern border, were bound to their King by a special agreement. The holder of such lands was obliged to go with his men, at the King's cost in the King's army when called upon to do so, with reasonable warning of such "conscription". This was called Pennaeth.

The estates inherited by Glyn Dwr were the subject of an inquisition in 1321 which reveals that the lands of Glyndyfrdwy, were held "of the King in chief" by the Welsh barony. As the land was in the county of Merioneth, the court at Harlech was responsible for ensuring that the holder of Glyndyfrdwy did not try to avoid his obligation. This particular agreement between King and baron was to prove important. It is also intriguing to note that Gruffydd ap Madog, Owen's grandfather, was mentioned in 1343 as one of the Welsh tenants who had not tendered homage to the new Prince of Wales, Edward III's son. Apparently Glyn Dwr's ancestor had not rushed to swear allegiance with any undue haste.

When ten-year-old Richard became King in 1377, Glyn Dwr was approximately eighteen. Although the war between England and France was temporarily suspended it was an uneasy time in Europe. Across the Channel another boy-king ascended the throne when Charles VI succeeded his father in 1380. Great social changes were occurring in England as an indirect result of the Black Death and its secondary cloud of infection in 1361-2 which had killed so many men that labour was scarce. The peasants discovered that they could charge more for their services although laws restricted their wages, and the earlier system of villeinage was crumbling as more and more workers either ran away from their bondage or were enfranchised by their lords to seek work as free men. In 1381 London was invaded by angry serfs and villains who refused to pay the Poll Tax, a levy which they felt was unjust and iniquitous. Led by Wat Tyler, the peasants murdered some of the King's ministers and burned the Savoy Palace, John of Gaunt's house in the Strand. The revolt failed after Richard persuaded the mob that he would give them what they asked.

There is some evidence that Glyn Dwr fought in the King's Scottish campaigns as one battle in 1385 is mentioned during the Chester trial of 1386. By this time the peasants had been forgotten and squabbles at court were developing into more serious rivalries, but the northern borders had to be defended against marauding Scots so Richard led a punitive force as far as Edinburgh, before returning to face a rebellion closer to home in 1387.

There are poems which record Glyn Dwr's success as a soldier written by the bards Iolo Goch and Gruffydd Llwyd. In one he is described as "Knight of the Glen", son of a famous father, at Berwick during this venture in Richard's army. Iolo describes his lord's courage and strength, fighting on with a broken lance, driving the Scots before him like wild goats. He wore a helmet with a scarlet feather and performed like a mighty warrior, bringing glory to his household. While these noble deeds were not noticed by Richard, who conferred no honours on Glyn Dwr, his faithful bard left no one in any doubt and some allowances must be made for poetic licence and exaggeration. Perhaps it was during this march that the Welsh baron made the acquaintance of the Percy of Northumberland family, and gained their respect. Later events indicate that Hotspur, Northumberland's son, regarded Glyn Dwr as an able soldier.

The Chester trial, which could be referred to as "Much Ado about Nothing", is famous not for the dispute itself but for the length of the proceedings. The records are a valuable source of information as the participants were members of great families who gave details of ages and pedigrees which prove their right to give evidence. When knights were covered from head to toe in armour, heraldic recognition was part of every young nobleman's education. On the battle-field a steelclad warrior's only identification would be his insignia, his colours and armorial banners which served to distinguish him from any other on the field. In the uproar and confusion of medieval combat it was difficult to decide which soldiers were on which side. This possibility of error in a general melee, often exploited by crafty leaders, helps to explain Shakespeare's use of "mistaken identity" in some of his battle-scenes. By dressing several knights in the same "colours" it was a simple procedure to produce half-a-dozen kings or celebrated warriors to mislead the enemy. When one was slain, another appeared.

The court of chivalry at Chester lasted almost five years, and it concerned a dispute over the coat-of-arms, "azure a bend or", which was claimed by Richard, Lord Scrope of Bolton and Robert Grosvenor of Hulme in Cheshire. Grosvenor's claim was supported by evidence and testimony from men of his own county and the neighbouring marches of Wales. The young lord of "Glendore" swore that he had seen Grosvenor bearing the coat-of-arms during their last sortie into Scotland. His younger brother Tudur, aged twenty-four "et pluis" added his evidence, as did other relatives and many young squires from the locality. Their names give sound indications as to the upper-class circles with which Glyn Dwr would be familiar. Geoffrey Chaucer, who gave his sworn statement less than a month after Glyn Dwr on 12th October, 1386, had been called because he had borne arms for twenty-seven years. He had accompanied Edward III to France in 1359 so this claim was true and, unlike the matter of ages, can be verified. Chaucer the writer was also a soldier; his connection with the House of Lancaster had ensured that he had led an itinerant and educational life. As a diplomat he had visited many countries, collecting experiences and meeting a wide variety of people which provided material for his *Canterbury Tales*. The son of a vintner, Chaucer himself displayed an illegal coat-of-arms, a red and white shield which some referred to disparagingly as the red and white of his family trade. Even humble tradesmen sought to impress as they prospered, and the Chaucer family was well-connected by marriage to the House of Lancaster, Chaucer's sister-in-law, Katherine Swynford becoming the third wife of John of Gaunt.

Many of the witnesses were called simply to substantiate that the coat-of-arms in question had previously been used on the battle-field over a period of years. Chaucer spoke on Scrope's behalf, as did many barons and nobles who were unfriendly towards King Richard. They too had been involved with the expedition to Scotland, alongside John of Gaunt. It would seem that even at this early stage Glyn Dwr found himself, in the courtroom, on the opposite side to the House of Lancaster.

In 1386 Gaunt left England to pursue a claim to the throne of Castile which prize, he declared, was his through marriage to a second wife, Constance, daughter of Pedro the Cruel, King of Castile and Leon. It was to be an unfulfilled dream, but his absence left King Richard free to rule England as he pleased without the restraining hand of Lancaster.

The recurring threat of a French invasion was met by the Earl of Arundel in 1387. Henry Bolingbroke was also in command of a large force during the winter of 1386-7 to help in the defence of England as a French fleet gathered to await good weather for the Channel crossing. Some historians insist that Glyn Dwr was present, either with Arundel or Bolingbroke, an assumption that seems highly probable. The man in charge of operations was Richard's favourite, Michael de la Pole, Earl of Suffolk, the son of a merchant who had risen to the office of Chancellor under the young King's patronage. His ineptness, which had almost resulted in disaster for England, caused a rift between the King and his Parliament when Pole was impeached and imprisoned by a council which included the Earl of Arundel.

After seeking the advice of some sympathetic judges,

Richard decided that the Council had acted illegally. By November the King had collected a small army of loyal followers from Cheshire with the intention of marching against his enemies, the men who had dared to imprison Pole, his very dear friend. Another of his favourites, Robert de Vere, Earl of Oxford, led men of Cheshire towards London to add strength to Richard's retaliation. He was met by the forces of Arundel, Warwick and Bolingbroke at Radcot Bridge.

The Merciless Parliament of 1388, and with Gloucester, Bolingbroke, Mowbray, Warwick and Arundel calling themselves the Lords Appellant, tried the King's favourites by the direct procedure of appealing them for treason; Pole and de Vere were exiled while others were executed. The King's circle of intimate friends was broken and scattered.

The Battle of Radcot Bridge was to have unforeseeable repercussions. Although the Lords Appellant were the victors, destroying the King's favourites whom they detested, it was Richard who eventually won the day – for a short time. He waited ten years for his revenge.

There has been endless speculation concerning Glyn Dwr's part during these important years. If he was indeed "squire" in Bolingbroke's retinue, or alternatively with the Earl of Arundel's household, then he may have been alongside either one of them at Radcot Bridge. But his feudal obligation was to the King. Only Cheshire supported Richard; other shires refused him support as they sided with the men of both the Lords and Commons. Glyn Dwr's lands were close enough to Cheshire to involve him on the King's side, but no one can prove where he was or indeed if he was on either side. It is, however, certain that Bolingbroke, as King, was more than usually antagonistic towards Glyn Dwr, a minor Welsh baron, displaying an attitude which indicates a long-standing dislike, or distrust. Loyalty to Richard survived in Cheshire and the Marches long after his death, and it was from there that Henry met most opposition after he had stolen the throne. If Glyn Dwr had served with Bolingbroke, but supported Richard, the events which were to transform the baron into a prince are more easily explained.

CHAPTER FIVE

Home and Family

"There dwells the lord of Powis land,
Who granteth every just demand.
Its likeness now I'll limn you out;
'Tis water-girdled wide about;
It shows a wide and stately door
Reached by a bridge the water o'er . . . "

Iolo Goch,
translated by
George Borrow.

SOME time during the period of early manhood Glyn Dwr married a lady called Margaret Hanmer from Flint, possibly in 1383 when he was twenty-four years old.

Margaret was the daughter of an important gentleman, Sir David Hanmer of Hanmer, whose distinguished legal career led to his appointment as a judge of the King's Bench in 1383. The Hanmer family was originally English, but long residence at Maelor in Flint had led to inter-marriage with their Welsh neighbours. This mingling of blood among border families was not at all unusual as boundaries were not as distinct as many imagine. There was no clear-cut dividing line to separate the two countries, and a century of peace had had its inevitable effect. The wealthy gentry of the marches, and the boroughs which had been established by Edward I, were a mixture of English and Welsh families whose main considerations were the preservation and enlargement of their estates rather than the purity of their blood.

When Sir David died in 1387, the affairs of his sons' estates were assigned to trustees who later transferred their duties to Glyn Dwr, obviously trusting his judgement and ability to look after the interests of Sir David's widow and children. Owen's brother-in-law, John Hanmer, was also a witness at the Chester trial. Owen's family and the Hanmers were obviously of similar wealth and prestige, respected within their community, and secure in their positions as the local leaders of society.

From the year of the trial until 1399, very little can be told of the young baron's life. Obviously he had lands and estates to supervise, and a family to keep him busy. His career was in the domestic arena, with the normal activities of a country gentleman to fill his days. He probably travelled a great deal between Carrog, Sycharth and South Wales, ensuring that his tenants were running their farms satisfactorily.

There is no indication that he was involved in any of the plots that were hatching against Richard, and it is unlikely that he sought involvement. He may have seen military service in Richard's name, as a soldier in the Irish expeditions of 1394-5. It would have been odd if such a distinguished young warrior had not been called upon to help his King when the troublesome rebels across the water were causing unrest. He did fight in Scotland during 1385, and the respect shown to the Welshman's prowess on the field by men such as Hotspur in later years indicates that Glyn Dwr must have gained military experience, and merit, at some time before Bolingbroke's bid for power.

He was a wealthy man by the standards of the time, since the estates he had inherited provided a good living. The Glen of the Water of the Dee, Glyndyfrdwy, is situated in an area of beautiful countryside between Llangollen and Corwen, close to Carrog where the River Dee flows alongside what is now the A5. This narrow glyn, or glen, separates the uplands of the Northern Clwydian range from the Berwyns which guard Bala. It was rough, wild country where life had barely changed from the early days of the Welsh princes, and the inhabitants had retained their Welsh identity. Although the lands of Glyndyfrdwy have recently been affected by encroaching tourism, the countryside and the people still retain that identity. It was fine hunting land which bred a hard, rural populace, far removed from the sumptuous court of Richard's London where Glyn Dwr had been educated.

Although Owen's title, Lord of Glyn Dwr, was inherited from this estate, his principal manor was at Sycharth in the parish of Llansilin on the southern side of the River Ceiriog and the Berwyn Mountains. This was the lordship of Cynllaith Owain, within easy distance of Oswestry and Chirk, centres of small but prosperous civilisation. At Sycharth the countryside was more amenable and the estates more profitable. The tenants of those fertile lands enjoyed a good living, and provided Owen with a healthy income.

Over a century before, in 1296, Gruffydd ap Madog the Prince of Northern Powys had died, leaving his lands to be divided between four sons as was customary in Wales by the ancient law of gavelkind. The lands included Glyndyfrdwy and Cynllaith. During the upheavals of 1282, at the time of Llywelyn the Last, these princes of Powys Fadog had supported the losing side. Their lands were divided among the Earl of Surrey, Roger Mortimer of Chirk, and Edward I's Queen, Eleanor of Castile. It seemed that the Welsh princes had lost everything.

However, by some means, Gruffydd Fychan, one of the four sons, placated the Earl of Surrey and in 1283 became the "tenant at will" of the lands of Glyndyfrdwy, his former inheritance. On his death the estates reverted to the Crown. Both Glyndyfrdwy and Cynllaith are mentioned in Queen Eleanor's will of 1290 as part of her estate. The lordship of the area had fallen to Reginald de Grey of Ruthin, but in 1293 a certain Thomas of Macclesfield was appointed as guardian to the lands of Gruffydd Fychan, "late tenant", since his son, the heir, was too young to manage the estates. By some unknown means the lands had become hereditary. Madog, the young son, wrote to King Edward I asking for a definite settlement, and by 1300 this Madog ap Gruffydd had become a baron of the Welsh March, owning the lands of Glyndyfrdwy and Cynllaith.

Not long afterwards, Madog died, leaving his young son Gruffydd to become a ward of John le Strange, the boy's father-in-law. There had been a very early marriage for the child. When le Strange died suddenly, the boy's inheritance fell into the hands of Edmund Hakluyt. The guardianship was bought by the Mortimers of Chirk. A legal battle followed as the boy reached the age to argue and lodge a formal claim, with the result that in 1321 young Gruffydd won back all his father's lands and became a baron in his own right by order of the King. As such he was required to provide men for the King's army whenever they were needed. In fact, he had regained the position held by his forefathers, with all the power and privileges of a Welsh prince.

The estates passed unharmed to his son, Gruffydd Fychan, the Younger, who continued the prudent management of the divided acres at Carrog and Sycharth. This Gruffydd also married wisely, for with his bride Helen came rich lands in

South Wales, the estates of Iscoed and Gwynionydd in Cardiganshire (Dyfed).

Helen was a daughter of the House of Deheubarth, a descendant of the great Lord Rhys who had ruled in South Wales as undisputed Prince. The son of this union was Owen Glyn Dwr. Thus the young man could claim descent from the princely rulers of Northern Powys, and from the royal rulers of Dinefwr in South Wales. It was this inheritance that won him such support as a Welsh leader. To his tenants he was more royal, and more real, than any of the rulers of England, particularly Henry Bolingbroke. The Welsh people had, and still have, great respect for genealogical claims.

We may imagine this young lord as a commanding personality, probably tall and fair-skinned as a result of his Celtic ancestry. The Northumberland followers of Cunedda who had populated Gwynedd were Celts of a different stature and complexion to those Iberian Celts on the western coasts of early Wales. He would be dressed in rich clothes, accustomed to wearing the fur-trimmed garments of brocade and silk which were fashionable at Richard's court. He would have fine horses, armour, weapons and all the accoutrements of a noble knight. His wife was probably more homely, grown plump after many confinements, also dressed in the fine clothes befitting her rank. She was obviously healthy as childbearing was a dangerous business in the fourteenth century. Henry Bolingbroke's wife, Mary de Bohun, was seventeen at the birth of their son Henry of Monmouth. This light-hearted young woman died at the age of twenty-four, after producing five more sons and daughters.

Lady Glyn Dwr was probably an expert household manager, a skill acquired after years of offering hospitality to their many friends and relatives. They were blessed with many children, most of whom apparently survived the ever-present dangers of infancy. Perhaps the settled life and comfortable existence in such a pleasant environment contributed to their survival. Mortality rates in the towns of England were dreadfully high, the cures for diseases often more harmful than the diseases themselves. There are references to six sons — Gruffydd, Madog and Maredudd, who played a part in the rebellion; and three more, Thomas, John and David about whom little is known. There were several daughters. Isabel is said to have married a Welshman, Adda ab Iorwerth Ddu, but there is scant information about them. Alice married John Scudamore of Holme Lacey. John held other estates in Herefordshire at Ewyas and Kentchurch which made him a neighbour of Roger Monnington of Monnington, the man who married Margaret. Another Hereford gentleman, John Crofts of Croft Castle married Janet, while Catherine remained at her father's home to become the wife of her father's prisoner, Edmund Mortimer. The names of Owen's daughters are given variously as Isabel, Elizabeth, Janet, Margaret, Catherine or Alice, and Jane. As the children escaped the later publicity, excepting those directly involved in the uprising, there seems to be no verifiable evidence to limit the number of offspring. Indeed, Glyn Dwr is mentioned as the father of others outside the matrimonial bed, but such claims are not uncommon where heroes are concerned.

There is information that Glyn Dwr's annual income was three hundred marks, a substantial amount which enabled him to maintain a large household with many retainers, while he lived the life of a great lord in some luxury.

His people were happy enough to work for him since he was not cruel or grasping like many of the other barons and Marcher Lords along the border. His ancestry was impeccable, and among the Welsh people his name commanded all the respect due to the son of an ancient and royal house.

Iolo Goch described Sycharth in great detail. The manor was surrounded by a moat over which a bridge led to the imposing gate-house. On the green hill were timber houses, built on pillars, which resembled the cloisters of Westminster. The roofs were tiled; the chimneys smoked, indicating the continual activity within as lavish meals were prepared for the many guests who frequently savoured Glyn Dwr's hospitality. The wardrobes were full of rich apparel, so full of gorgeous materials that they were like shops in Cheapside. Close by stood a mill, among other small buildings such as a stone pigeon-house. There was a rabbit warren and a heronry, and the whole complex of buildings exuded warmth, joy and a welcome from Owen's delightful wife.

In the enlightened atmosphere of such a home the children of this intelligent man would have been sharp and inquisitive, eager to hear the news and songs of the bards who travelled Wales, visitors to Sycharth who were certain of good food and a warm reception.

These bards held a high position in Welsh society, and some

thought very highly of themselves, with their ability to glorify the deeds of their ancestors, and their current protectors, in wonderful verse. The composition of Welsh verse demanded a high degree of skill, as definite patterns and metre play an essential part in the poem. The alliterative poetry of Early English writers had been replaced by more fluid forms as the language developed, but in Wales the method has continued to the present day. Bards often claimed the power to see into the future, an attribute that would guarantee an esteemed position among the superstitious peasants. Long ago the Romans had eliminated the Druids in Wales, realising that their influence was dangerous. Some remnant of that distant religion lived on in the bards who travelled widely like the early Druid teachers, bringing news and rumour to the countryside. Perhaps some of them did have the gift of second-sight; a belief in prophecies was not restricted to the lower classes. Glyn Dwr himself was held to have magical powers during later years, a rumour that he used to advantage. Patrons had their own "household bards", or bardd teulu, who ensured that successful enterprises were recorded and enshrined in verse. The poems could be chanted or sung to the accompaniment of the harp to entertain guests as they lounged at the fireside after a hearty meal. Music was popular with all classes both in Wales and England, while the appreciation of poetry was universal.

Glyn Dwr certainly had wide horizons, and his interests probably included alchemy, astrology and an awareness of contemporary theories concerning heavenly phenomena. There were disturbing new religious ideas to discuss as heretical preachers stalked the land, preaching the word of Wycliffe and the Lollards. The new English literature must have been known and appreciated by a cultured man such as Glyn Dwr. There were countless tales of chivalry, love and noble deeds, written by men who drew freely on the wealth of talent and stirring tales of Italy and France.

We may picture Owen enjoying the life of similar lords, perfecting his skill with weapons, hunting, flying falcons, perhaps teaching his young sons as they grew up in the delightful manor of Sycharth. He would be eager to learn from visitors, adding to his knowledge of current affairs during the uneasy peace with France. The continual quarrels with Ireland and Scotland would not have caused great alarm in the lord's household, although his absence would have been mourned. As a minor baron Glyn Dwr probably did his feudal duty and returned as soon as possible to the peace and security of Sycharth. When the English nobles fought their King, although Glyn Dwr was acquainted with the protagonists he was not directly concerned with the House of Lancaster, or any of the others, and owed them no allegiance. His life as a country landowner was far removed from the intrigues and jealousies of the court. When Henry Bolingbroke was exiled in 1398 it must have seemed that Richard was firmly in control; even those who sympathised with Henry kept their thoughts to themselves. It was not the first time that a King's enemies, or friends, had been disgraced, removed or firmly dealt with either temporarily or permanently.

In 1397 an entry in the registers of Pope Boniface IX reveals that the Lord of Glyn Dwr and his wife were granted the services of a confessor "in the hour of death". Obviously the Welsh family had more important matters to deal with. This indult would have been important when Heaven and Hell were very real places in the minds of God-fearing men and women. The dreadful vision of the Inferno conjured up so graphically by Dante in the *Divine Comedy* would have been well-known to literate men of the fourteenth century. Langland's *Vision of Piers Plowman* was written during the reign of Richard II, describing Man's search for Heaven and the true Christ. Confusion within the Church itself, and the grasping immoral life of some of the clergy, were matters which could not alter the devout religious beliefs of the people. Hell meant everlasting perdition and Heaven was the home of Christ; it was a simple choice. The concern for salvation which Glyn Dwr obviously felt seems at variance with the later belief that he was a magician who could control the elements and use the powers of witchcraft to assist his struggle against the English. For a man of his class and position it was, however, normal practice to ensure a comfortable after-life by communicating with the Pope who was, after all, God's representative on Earth.

As the course of events in England swirled towards an unavoidable weir, the Lord of Glyndyfrdwy was more concerned with domestic affairs, far from the turbulence in his manor at Sycharth or hunting at Carrog. The news of Bolingbroke's disgrace must have reached every corner of the kingdom, but the populace was more worried about the increasingly heavy taxation imposed by Richard as he sought to replenish the coffers which were always empty. Free from restraint, now the absolute monarch, Richard punished those counties where support had been refused ten years previously by fining them for their disloyalty.

Even the King's most dedicated followers in Cheshire and the Marches must have grumbled at the cost, but there were rumours of a new expedition to Ireland, under Richard's command, to provide hopes of employment and wages, and the permanent army of Cheshire archers was strengthened both for their sovereign's peace of mind and for the renewal of hostilities. It is likely that the men of Wales were placed on the alert and instructed to prepare themselves for the Irish excursion.

The castles and garrisons of Edward I had enforced peace in Wales; large areas of Welsh soil were in the hands of English barons. The sons of Wales were educated at English universities, to return as gentlemen with English manners and customs. Yet the Welsh way of life continued in homes such as Sycharth, where Glyn Dwr maintained a Neuadd in the old way offering hospitality, entertainment and friendship to his visitors. They spoke the old language, although many, like Glyn Dwr, had learned Latin and French in addition to English. Loyal to the King of England, the Welsh retained a more deep-rooted loyalty to their own countrymen, to their own lords like Glyn Dwr who was descended from a line of rulers who were accustomed to power. Centuries before, the Northumbrians had established their supremacy over earlier settlers in Wales. From the time of Cunedda, the great families of Gwynedd had developed as a race apart from the tenants and lower classes they controlled. Great reverence was attached to the names of those early princes whose deeds were recounted by the bards, each memory enshrined in glowing verse. Proud of their history, proud of their heroes, the Welsh lived uncomfortably under their English King. Beneath the affability and acceptance lay an unseen mixture of resentment, betrayed by small eruptions which were of no consequence. Among a subjugated people there will always be one or two men who seek to overturn the established order. The conquering power calls them rebels; the vanquished call them patriots.

Intent on the Irish problem, Richard remained unaware that the Welsh were dissatisfied with English rule. Although the uprising became the main concern of his successor, the discontent had been brewing for a long time. The arrogant Marcher Lords, of Norman descent, were often harsh masters. Large areas of Wales suffered under their dictatorship. Those Welsh who were fortunate to be the tenants of Welsh landlords managed to keep alive the spirit of their ancestors, retaining the beliefs and culture of their distinctive race.

The suggestion that Glyn Dwr's country rose in rebellion because of a petty disagreement between neighbours is perpetuated in many accounts of this period. To accept this is to ignore a hundred years of English dominance over a defeated nation.

When John of Gaunt died in February, 1399, his enormous wealth and estates provided Richard with the finance he so desperately needed. The King travelled through Wales on his way to the Irish wars, leaving behind a small force to deal with any minor disturbances that might occur. There were no preparations for a major upheaval as Richard saw no danger from within his realm. The man he had feared most, old Gaunt, was dead; Lancaster's traitorous son was safely across the Channel, without lands or money. When, in August, Henry re-entered England and marched triumphantly across the country to Bristol with the intention of claiming his stolen estates, Richard's followers in Wales were hastily gathered together to meet the unexpected threat. While the Welsh had always professed loyalty to the King, they offered no real resistance when Richard most needed their support. The "loyal force" disintegrated and disappeared with miraculous haste. In the words of Shakespeare's Welsh captain, "Farewell; our countrymen are gone and fled."

CHAPTER SIX

Changes

"My lord of Hereford here, whom you call king,
Is a foul traitor to proud Hereford's king;
And if you crown him, let me prophesy, —
The blood of English shall manure the ground . . ."

William Shakespeare.
King Richard II
Act IV scene i.

GLYN Dwr's tranquil life as a country land-owner was to end in 1399, when England's King suffered an ignominious fate at the hands of ambitious men. The whole of Britain was soon to seethe as long-held feelings of resentment finally broke the surface. The usurpation of the sanctified monarch signalled dark forces which were to cast a shadow over the whole of Henry's brief and blood-spattered reign.

Richard II had lived royally, totally unaware of the great poverty and hardship endured by most of his subjects. Probably he was not intentionally unfeeling, since most monarchs lived a life sheltered from the nastier side of reality. The King's court during the last ten years of his reign was the setting for sumptuous pageantry, where elegance and style were appreciated above all else. The gorgeously-dressed lords and ladies loved music and dancing; Richard himself adored extravagant clothes, fine jewellery and entertainment, surrounded by his admiring friends. They consumed incredible amounts of food. Increased trade and new contacts through Venice meant that exotic spices from the East were available to tempt jaded appetites and embellish the more traditional fare of England. The palace cookery-book contained many recipes for dishes such as minced pheasant, or oysters in Greek wine; cloves and cinnamon flavoured the meats while ginger and sugar were added to delight the palate. There were wines from France, Germany and the Mediterranean. No doubt Richard never knew where the food came from, or how many peasants suffered to provide the luxuries he took for granted. Wat Tyler's annoying little interruption was casually forgotten; the King had no wish to meet his subjects at such close quarters again. When the royal entourage travelled, it was with suitable ceremony to the castle or manor of his choice. The cost to the lord who had to provide nourishment for such a guest was often crippling, and many hearts must have sunk when Richard decided to honour his nobles with the royal presence.

Some of the finest illuminated manuscripts and intricate tapestries were created during Richard's reign. English literature, written in the new English language, emerged as a vibrant, exciting alternative to the dull Latin treatises of the earlier years. Poets such as Chaucer read their poems aloud to the richly-clad, and appreciative, lords and ladies. Men of intellect were familiar with the great literature of France and Italy. Dante, Petrarch and Boccaccio were universally admired, and their stories formed the basis for many English adaptations. French romances emphasised chivalry and courtly love as fictional knights and ladies pursued their often tragic lives, attaining true happiness and a place in Heaven after countless tribulations. The chronicler Jehan Froissart* visited the court to bring Richard a copy of his latest poems.

There were tournaments to attend, where young knights could demonstrate their military skills and horsemanship in competition for the favours of beautiful damsels who knew nothing of the horrors of actual warfare. It was all a great charade, and an excuse for festivities.

Richard's first wife, Anne of Bohemia, the daughter of Emperor Charles IV, had brought new customs to the English court. Her death in 1394 caused the King much grief, which was partially assuaged by his marriage to the daughter of Charles VI, of France, the child princess Isabella. Her retinue brought a considerable French influence to the court in 1396 and a truce between the two countries hastened the exchange of ideas and fashions.

Many soldiers had travelled widely, and their accounts of experiences in distant countries would be listened to with eagerness and disbelief. The travels of Sir John Mandeville, written during Edward III's reign, show that travellers had explored as far as India and China. Mandeville declared that

*Froissart's *Chroniques de France et d'Angleterre* covered the period 1325-1400 in France and England.

his men had served the Sultan of Babylon, at war with the Bedouins; he wrote that they had served the Great Chan of the Tartars of Cathay. This account, describing in detail such a variety of exotic countries and inhabitants, was available in Latin, French and English so that everyone could read about the marvels of Tartary, Persia, Libya, Ethiopia, India and fabulous Cathay. While it would appear that Sir John Mandeville did not himself visit these far-flung places and gleaned much of his information from authentic travellers, the book was undeniably popular. Dispute concerning the authorship of these tales has not detracted from their worth, or diminished the importance of this compilation of experiences within fourteenth century literature.

Old campaigners could have told incredible tales of the Black Prince and England's victories abroad. For the wealthy it was a stimulating and enjoyable hiatus, with England at peace; or at least there was calm on the surface. For the peasants it hardly mattered, as all kings demanded rents and taxes; that some were more considerate, or cruel, were facts of life. He, the King, was still God's anointed, and if God's choice appeared misguided it was not for peasants to argue. You fought and died for your King, or you worked and died. It was all the same. However, if your immediate landlord, to whom you paid rents and for whom you worked, decided to take up arms against the King, for his own reasons, then you followed your leader.

Sumptuous living requires unlimited resources, and Richard's weakness was a total lack of financial acumen. From childhood he had been spoilt, accustomed to extravagance and shielded from the poverty of ordinary people. He had been used as a figure-head since his accession, and state affairs had been left in the hands of powerful men who were only too happy to serve a boy-king who was easily swayed and manipulated. When he was old enough to realise that a King could use his power, Richard offended many of his nobles by promoting favourites to positions of importance. New taxes were introduced which caused great hardship as the new men tried to extort yet more money from the suffering people. The nobles had reacted by organising themselves into a strong faction which ensured their victory at Radcot Bridge, but by the year 1398 Richard was strong enough to order the deaths of those who had hurt his personal friends, and the humiliation he had endured was revenged. With his enemies executed, murdered or in exile, Richard the absolute monarch decided to lead an army into Ireland, to win glory for himself and to prove to his subjects that he, the King, was firmly in control. His advisors, if they had any influence, must have been singularly ill-informed as to the situation in England.

Henry Bolingbroke was a formidable soldier, respected and, perhaps, feared. He had grown up in an atmosphere of wealth and power, in the security of castles dominated by his father whose progeny were remarkable, and clever. During Richard's adolescence, John of Gaunt had been the power behind the throne. As leader of the league of magnates who governed England until the King reached maturity, the Duke of Lancaster was king in everything but name. Although unpopular with many, he certainly wielded unchallenged authority. After the death in 1369 of his first wife, Blanche, Henry's mother, John of Gaunt married Constance, daughter of Pedro the Cruel of Castile, with the hope of claiming a throne for himself. He made an unsuccessful bid for Castile and Leon and returned to England to content himself with his established position as first lord of the land. He caused a great scandal by marrying in 1396, his former mistress, Katherine Swynford, a lady who had been governess to his daughters but who had also produced several children while in the Lancaster household. In 1397, Richard legitimised the children, the Beauforts, and the House of Lancaster gained intelligent, gifted heirs who were to make their own mark on English history.

When Lancaster died in 1399, Richard lost no time in confiscating all his wealth and property. By this action he broke the promise made to the banished Bolingbroke that he should succeed to his father's possessions. In addition the King's loyalty to an old and revered noble was non-existent; perhaps he had spent all his life in fear of the great soldier whose material assets were so enormous. It was a golden opportunity to grab sudden wealth, riches that would enable him to write his own name in the annals of history. The King sought glory and the respect of his people, and a soldier was admired by everyone.

The Lancaster heir was not so easily robbed. When he arrived at Ravenspur, accompanied by Thomas, Archbishop Arundel, his forces were soon joined by England's great family armies. The new Earl of Arundel, whose father had been beheaded in 1398; the Earl of Northumberland; the Nevilles and all the Lancastrian supporters of Gaunt's many castles swelled the ranks of Henry's formidable force. Many of these landowners must have feared the same treatment from Richard. If great Gaunt's estates could be snatched so avariciously then no-one's inheritance was safe. Compared to Richard, Henry was strong and forceful; many must have felt that they were choosing the winning side even before events could prove them right. Unedifying rumours and scurrilous tales of Richard's personal habits and preferences for young men, substantiated by the fact that he had produced no heirs, no doubt encouraged men of unquestionable tastes to hurry to the side of virile Henry Bolingbroke.

From Bristol, where Henry dealt with some of Richard's cronies, the army marched northwards, unopposed. The King sailed across the Irish Sea to Milford Haven (Milffwrd) with part of his army to meet this internal threat. Finding that there was no military support in Wales he went in disguise to Conwy Castle for safety. It was a cold welcome. The Earl of Northumberland presented Henry's grievances, persuading the King that there was no danger to his person or his position; the Lancaster heir sought only the return of his legal inheritance. Virtually unprotected in the huge, empty fortress, Northumberland's assurances must have sounded extremely hollow to the King's disbelieving ears.

With little option, a small royal entourage travelled to Flint Castle where a meeting had been arranged with Henry to discuss his claim. The size of the Lancaster army, and the renown of the powerful allies who accompanied Bolingbroke had frightened away any hesitant opposition from the Welsh or from any foolhardy Cheshire archers who may have lingered in the district.

For Richard it was the end of an unsatisfactory reign, lightened only by intervals of heady freedom and the gaiety of the court. The handsome young man, sensitive to beauty but self-centred and altruistic, was compelled to bend his proud head before Henry Bolingbroke. Shakespeare's account of Richard's abdication partly exonerates Henry from blame, and the deposed King's terrible sadness at his parting from the young Queen arouses our pity and sympathy. The ceremony at Westminster describes Richard's voluntary submission. England's crown is handed over by a defeated, bewildered man, a "mockery-king of snow" standing before the "sun of Bolingbroke".

Richard was taken to Pontefract Castle in Yorkshire, for safe-keeping. He was not seen again, alive. Henry placed the crown on his own head, and then asked Parliament to approve; he had regained his inheritance, and added the whole kingdom as compensation. With the accession of Henry IV the old order was changed forever. Like the early rulers of Britain he had taken the crown by force of arms, and the Plantagenet line ended in the dark dungeons of Pontefract.

Glyn Dwr would certainly have known of these treacherous events as there would have been much activity in his own area close to Rhuddlan and Flint. He was known personally to Henry, to Arundel and to the Northumberland Percies. He also knew Richard. We may imagine that his loyalties must have been with the true King, whatever his faults, as his own line of descent from a royal house was of considerable importance to him. It is hard to believe that he would have joined the usurper, whose grievances were genuine enough, but whose claim to the throne was not legitimate. Later events show that Henry owed the Welshman no favours. Yet if Glyn Dwr were present on any of the occasions when Richard was in North Wales, in desperate need of assistance, he must have taken the prudent course and sided with no-one. Perhaps the younger Percy tried to persuade him that their cause was justified; perhaps Richard's adherents hoped that he would support them. Whatever the situation, Glyn Dwr's name was still to be written on the pages of time. He obviously learned the lesson exemplified by Henry's revolt. It is not known whether Shakespeare's reference to Glendower at this time was merely a dramatic device, perhaps to link events with the action of subsequent plays, or whether it was information from an historical source. In Act III, scene i, of *Richard II,* Henry's forces are at Bristol, having captured the King's supporters Bushy and Green. They are shown, and expect, no mercy. Henry makes it clear that the innocent Queen must be assured of her safety, and adds;

> "*. . . Come, Lords, away,*
> *To fight with Glendower and his complices*
> *Awhile to work, and after holiday.*"

It may be that the playwright was simply using the name of one Welshman, known to his audience, to represent all Welshmen who were in Richard's service. Alternatively, Glyn Dwr may have been with Richard's army in Ireland, instructed to return to his native land with orders to halt Henry's progress. Welsh tactics at a later date indicate a knowledge of Irish methods which may have been learned at first hand, and the patriots of Ireland might well have touched a nerve in Welsh hearts. The rebels of Ireland would never accept English domination.

During 1399 in the months following Richard's abdication, Glyn Dwr registered various grievances with the English Parliament. The complaints concerned the theft of some of his land, and he must have hoped for a favourable result from the King whose position had been won as a result of a similar theft.

The case should have been heard at a meeting of the Parliament in the spring of 1400, but it was not important enough to occupy the time of busy Englishmen. Trevor, Bishop of St Asaph, is reported to have warned that it was unwise to provoke such a highly-respected Welshman, who might be a minor baron to the great lords of the King's circle, but who was important to the people of his own area. The Bishop received a scornful reply to this diplomatic intercession.

A few months earlier, during the Christmas period, there had been a plot to murder King Henry. Many of Richard's friends had been deprived of their titles and estates when the new ruler assumed his throne, although their lives had been spared. Hoping to deceive Henry by preparing a Twelfth Night celebration in his honour, a group of Richard's followers planned an assassination attempt whereby they hoped to seize the usurper, kill him and free Richard. The plot was betrayed and the conspirators captured; soon afterwards Richard "died". Henry had seen the danger and eliminated it. If Glyn Dwr was known to be loyal to Richard, or if men such as Lord Grey, the man who had stolen the land, insinuated that the Welshman was disloyal to Henry, then it is easy to understand why the lawsuit failed.

In the summer of 1400, perhaps ruffled by the events of the Bolingbroke rebellion, there were many small disturbances among the people of Cheshire and along the Welsh border. Men refused to believe that Richard was dead, and it was easy to convince the simple countryfolk that they should rally to their former King who would appear among them in person when the time was ripe. They were not convinced, nor could they accept, that God's anointed had been murdered.

Other disturbances in the neighbourhood of Glyndyfrdwy were caused by a roving bandit, Gruffydd ap Dafydd ap Gruffydd. After he was almost caught by the crafty ruse of the Bishop of St Asaph who enticed him to Oswestry by promising him an honest position as bailiff of the Arundel lordship, the criminal sought safety among the people of Dyffryn Clwyd. Wild Dafydd ignored all the established laws of ownership, particularly if the owner happened to be Lord Grey of Ruthin whose territories included Dyffryn Clwyd. He proceeded to steal horses and supplies, and generally made a nuisance of himself, safely hidden by the Welsh tenants who no doubt enjoyed the tales of his exploits against their hated lord.

Reginald Grey, Lord of Ruthin, had ruled Dyffryn Clwyd since 1388. It was a hereditary title, with estates granted at the time of Edward I. At this period the two neighbours were about the same age, but Grey was a peer in Parliament, a former Governor of Ireland, a great land-owner, and a close friend of Henry IV. He had officiated at the Coronation celebrations, and had become a member of the King's Council. He was not a man to pay much heed to the irritating Welsh nobody whose lands adjoined the vast Ruthin property. That summer there were far more pressing matters which required his attention.

The irrepressible Dafydd pursued his career and even corresponded directly with Lord Grey, threatening him with reciprocal action should any of his countrymen be punished for aiding and abetting. Grey replied by threatening Dafydd with hanging, should he be caught, along with any who assisted him.

After any military campaign, some men are left to wander, without homes or employment. In the years which followed this century's wars, many soldiers found themselves washed up on the beach of peacetime like so much damaged flotsam which no-one could use. In Wales, when Richard's followers dispersed, some returned to their families while others went to join other armies, or to seek work wherever it was available. Others, uprooted from their homes at an early age, unskilled in anything but warfare, were left to wander the countryside. When honest work was unavailable they were obliged to beg or steal food in order to exist. Not unnaturally they robbed the wealthy English rather than their equally poor countrymen. For such men it was safer to form groups, and small roving bands of hungry felons were a constant source of irritation to the landlords of the Marches.

Those whose job it was to protect people from the robbers were occasionally sympathetic to the criminals, as the Welsh have large families with many connections. The Welsh-born officers of the King's shires were not likely to arrest their uncles' cousins or their nephews' sons.

The horse-thief who wrote so tauntingly to Lord Grey was only one more outrageous robber than many others, and more literate. In the atmosphere of lawlessness which followed the usurpation of the English throne, insecurity and hunger were creating disloyal ideas in the minds of many Welshmen. The disaffection spread, from the firesides of disgruntled peasants to the halls of their own lords; autocratic English landowners ignored the murmurs of discontent at their peril. For too long the people of Wales had obeyed English masters.

When preparations were being made for an expedition to Scotland in 1400, Lord Grey was in command of the general muster which obliged local barons to send men to fight in the King's army. By accident or design, Grey did not inform Glyn Dwr of the royal command, and the Welshman did not send his quota to join the assembled force. Their absence enabled Grey to inform Henry that the Welsh baron was a traitor. The feudal agreement stated clearly that sufficient notice must be given; soldiers could not be armed and provisioned in a few days. By withholding the information, Grey had left Owen with no option but to refuse.

In retrospect, the events of that summer which left the Lord of Glyndyfrdwy with a relatively free hand might arouse suspicion in cynical minds. The master of Ruthin had appropriated some of Glyn Dwr's land which bordered Grey's estates near Derwen, south of Ruthin. As a close friend of the King, Grey must have been very sure that his claims would take precedence over those of a traitorous Welshman, especially if he insinuated that Glyn Dwr's sympathies lay with Richard, or Richard's heir. Secure in his position at the new court, Grey established ownership by force, as Marcher Lords had always done. Glyn Dwr's attempts to obtain justice through an English court, using the legal means he would naturally follow as a result of his early education, were unsuccessful. Grey's insistance that the Welsh baron was untrustworthy, or a traitor, because he had dared to challenge the mighty earl's actions, persuaded Parliament to grant the Lord of Ruthin powers to deal with the malcontent in his own fashion, by force. Obviously Grey had much to gain. The lands of Glyndyfrdwy were valuable. By eliminating the Welshman, the estates would be forfeit to Grey; and the King's friend was greedy, as well as being malicious. The possibility of yet more lands was not a chance to be missed.

Grey was so powerful that many of the lesser barons along the Marches were afraid of his ambition. Neighbouring Welsh landowners in particular must have feared for their property if Grey was permitted to steal the lands of the Lord of Glyndyfrdwy. They resented this arrogant, English noble, just as they had always resented English interference of any description. For a hundred years they had served an English master, living uneasily under English law. The changes that had taken place in England now showed them that what had been accepted philosophically could be changed drastically by direct action. When the laws are broken by those in high positions, then the rule of law itself begins to break down.

The Welsh people still spoke the Welsh language. Their way of life had remained almost tribal, and they regarded their own lords as true Welsh princes. Families were closely linked, by marriage and custom. As a race, they had not been diluted like the Saxons who had integrated with their Norman conquerors. They were not as sophisticated as their English counterparts, whose cities and towns had brought new ideas, new standards and a wider outlook as trade increased. The Welsh were not merchants and tradespeople, they were mostly farming-stock who lived close to the land, close to their relatives. Their communities were more closed, untouched by foreign influences, their harsh lives leaving little time for merry-making other than occasional festivities. They were proud of their heritage, and their history, reminded of their past constantly by the bards whose songs perpetuated the memory of a more glorious era. The bards were ardent nationalists who were eager to make the people aware of their former importance, reminding them of their heroic princes who had defeated English armies. It was part of their code to maintain links with the past by reciting the genealogical evidence which proved the ancient claims of their patrons, men descended from Britons and Romans whose right to live and own lands could be traced far beyond the claims of the newcomers.

In the year 1400, Glyn Dwr was forty-one. He had royal blood in his veins. He was courageous, courteous, generous, and proud. The series of unrelated incidents during the early months of this new century were like tiny sparks blowing in the winds that swept the rugged terrain of North Wales. The minor uprisings along the Cheshire border; the antics of a rough bandit who stole English horses and laughed at the uproar; and the high-handed actions of Lord Grey were to prod the unrecognised twinges of latent patriotism. By September of 1400, the twinges had developed into growing pains which were to culminate in a momentous decision. No doubt the idea grew slowly, nourished by news of other incidents, brought into the open at last by men who recognised, and wanted, a chance to settle with the English once and for all.

Henry was fighting in Scotland. Lord Grey's omission to inform Glyn Dwr of the muster meant that the Welsh baron's men were still in Wales, a circumstance that may or may not have been the result of spite or, alternatively, Welsh intention. On 16th September, the King's army was returning from the northern battle-fields. No doubt his men were anticipating a peaceful winter in their respective homes. It must have been quite a shock for Henry to discover that his Welsh subjects in the West were going to cause trouble, in an area where there had been no opposition for a century. With his tired forces he marched angrily towards the stronghold of Shrewsbury, eager to settle this petty revolt of treacherous Welsh scoundrels.

Had he been able to read the omens and see into the future, Henry would not have been so confident. His reign was to be one long struggle, a continuous battle against enemies and former friends. The hollow crown was to rest heavily on his head, and the optimistic plans for a purifying crusade had to be postponed.

CHAPTER SEVEN

The New Prince of Wales

"Undaunted warrior, for thy country's weal
Scorning the hurtling shaft, the piercing steel;
With thy raw levies fronting without fear
The Marchers' serried ranks, the Norman's spear."

Sir Lewis Morris.

ON 16th September, 1400, Owen Glyn Dwr was at his manor of Glyndyfrdwy at Carrog. After Lord Grey's attacks on his lands he was no doubt ensuring that there were no more armed raids against his people, or against himself. While Grey was absent, accompanying Henry in Scotland, it was an ideal opportunity to restore the balance.

There must have been strong motives to drive Glyn Dwr to take the next irrevocable step. His reaction to Grey's attacks was to set in motion a chain of events which resembled those earlier rebellions led by Welsh leaders against King John, Henry III and the indomitable Edward I. It has been established that Glyn Dwr was a highly intelligent and cultured man, a promising soldier who had spent several years among the English, both as a student and as a squire in the service of the King, or the King's nobles. He was a well-loved baron of the Welsh royal-line, highly regarded by prominent English leaders. His actions of this autumn appear uncharacteristic of a man well acquainted with the law, and of a peaceful citizen. Unlike many of his countrymen, he had not shown signs of a hasty temper, or open hostility to his English neighbours. When provoked by Lord Grey he had taken legal steps to regain his property, through the proper procedures of Parliament.

Shakespeare credited Glyn Dwr with second-sight, or at least magical powers and a belief in prophecy. The facts seem to show that he must have felt that he was the chosen leader of his people, the true Prince of the Cymry who could not fail in this desperate enterprise. He must have known only too well the strength of the English army; he had seen Henry in action. Others have insisted that strange portents heralded this new leader, placing him in the same category as Jesus Christ and King Arthur whose births were accompanied by heavenly phenomena. It seems more likely that Glyn Dwr was visited not by visions, but by resentful Welshmen who catalogued their grievances, who disliked Henry IV and the new aristocracy of powerful nobles surrounding the throne, and who sought satisfaction while Henry was busy elsewhere. They would have been angry at English interference in their affairs, anxious to hold on to their lands when it seemed that some of the more ambitious earls were nibbling away at the border counties. More hot-tempered neighbours probably urged Glyn Dwr to stand up and fight for his countrymen when they were being maltreated and cheated by the English. The merchants of the boroughs were successful businessmen who seemed to acquire riches with little effort, at the expense of Welsh customers. It is not difficult to imagine how small resentments and jealousies must have built up between the prosperous English and the Welsh peasantry. Doubtless the bards sang songs of their ancestors who had lived as free men under the Good King, Hywel Dda, or as warriors in Llywelyn's army when Wales had been a united kingdom for the Welsh. There would have been many to point out that Glyn Dwr himself was a descendant of such heroes, yet he was doing nothing to protect his people. Waving pieces of paper in Parliament was going to achieve nothing.

Patriotism was a word the Welsh had not used for a century, but during those years of English rule and English laws, the infiltration of English settlers and the might of English castles, the Cymry had maintained a separate way of life and a language. Shakespeare's Lady Mortimer, Glyn Dwr's daughter, spoke no word of English. Since the days of Edward I the two nations had lived side by side in sullen peace, while underneath the surface the hatred had remained.

If they needed an example, Scotland was providing one. There were many similarities between the Welsh and the Scots, and both nations disliked the affluent, arrogant English. After a short period of peace, the men of Scotland were once again attacking the rich lordships along the frontier of the North, Glyn Dwr himself had had some experience of fighting in Scotland, alongside English soldiers. The raiders were adept at making quick forays, seizing hostages and booty, before disappearing into the mists. It was almost impossible to overcome such mercurial opposition, but the English generally succeeded in driving the brigands back as far as Edinburgh before returning to the comfort of their own castles. This constant battle with the Scots followed an established pattern; nobody won and nobody lost. Negotiations would then follow when hostages were traded for large sums of money.

The Scots had never accepted Edward I's domination as the Welsh had done at the end of the thirteenth century. Although similar castles had been built at strategic points to control their subjugated country, the Scots had risen to the call of Sir William Wallace and defeated the hated English at Stirling Bridge in 1297. Edward's retaliation at Falkirk in 1298 had seemed to conquer the northerners, but the fervour inspired by Wallace could not be quenched. In 1306, under the leadership of Robert Bruce, the Scots drove their enemies back over the border yet again. Edward I had died at the northern limits of his kingdom as he attempted to lead his army back into Scotland.

The battle of Bannockburn in 1314, when Edward II's disastrous leadership resulted in ignominious defeat for the English, ensured that Scotland remained a separate country. Edward III's attempts to conquer the unruly race were equally unsuccessful, and King David, the son of Robert Bruce, established himself firmly on the throne with assistance from friendly France. Marcher Lords, such as the Percies, tried to prevent invasions into their territory, but the Scots never ceased to fight for the border lands. They did not have to obey English laws or bend the knee to English earls as the Welsh did. While Chaucer was writing of jolly pilgrims and dreams of the Temple of Venus, the Archdeacon of Aberdeen, John Barbour, was writing *Bruce* to remind his people of their glorious past, keeping alive the bright vision of liberty and nationalism.

> *"Ah, Freedom is a noble thing;*
> *Freedom makes man to have liking;*
> *Freedom all solace to man gives;*
> *He lives at ease that freely lives."*

When the collaborators met at Carrog that September, they were armed and ready. They were able to assure their leaders that there was a Cause, and there was a populace eager and willing to do battle. News of general unrest in Wales reached Henry in Scotland, as letters were sent by worried landowners that the unruly peasantry were creating disturbances. There were even rumours that the Scots were planning to land a force at Barmouth (Abermaw), to march through Wales and attack Henry from the rear. This plan had been discovered by the constable of Harlech Castle who mistrusted the local Welsh gentry and believed that the scheme would soon be put into operation. Glyn Dwr may have called his friends together originally to reclaim his own lands from Grey, and with no ulterior motive. As it happened, at that time, the men of Wales needed but one indication that someone would make a move, and the news that Glyn Dwr was contemplating action would have spread through North Wales on the wings of welcome rumour.

It may be true that he visualised a new beginning for the Cymry, with himself as the Chosen One. Glyn Dwr was proclaimed Prince of Wales and he assumed the role without fear or argument: after all, he was a prince of Wales by hereditary right. Driven by frustrations, persuaded by close friends and relatives, possibly influenced by predictions, the domesticated gentleman had chosen to become the Warrior Prince.

The assembled patriots, called conspirators by the English, included Glyn Dwr's brother Tudur, his son Gruffydd, and two of his wife's brothers, Gruffydd and Philip Hanmer. His sister's husband, Robert Puleston was there, and the Dean of St Asaph, Hywel Kyffin. From Powys Fadog came the Dean's nephews, Ieuan Fychan and Gruffydd ab Ieuan, together with Madog of Eyton.

A certain John Astwick was present, and a prophetic bard called Crach Ffynant, The Scab, who probably came from the area of Cynllaith. Doubtless there were others of lesser-known families in the neighbourhood, eager Welshmen waiting to rally to the Cause. This mixture of those true-blooded Welshmen with others of English descent is not incompatible as all were linked by family and a common bond of hatred for Grey or other Marcher Lords. It was not only the Welsh who were subservient. Glyn Dwr's own men, drawn from his estates, would naturally follow their leaders anywhere, against any foe, and they may have been armed already to go to Scotland, although the summons had arrived belatedly.

By 18th September, 1400, they had sufficient forces to march on Ruthin, gathering followers along the journey.

Around the castle of Ruthin a thriving township had developed, along the pattern of many others throughout Wales since the introduction of English boroughs after the Treaty of Rhuddlan. Increased prosperity and trade had led to the regular markets and Fair Days which marked the calendar of English towns, many of which continue today. As the carefree townsfolk were preparing for their annual fair of St Matthews' Day, held on 21st September, Glyn Dwr's men attacked the unsuspecting inhabitants and burnt the houses of Ruthin to the ground. This swift and devastating sortie, to destroy Lord Grey's property, was in direct retaliation, striking at the heart of the earl's little "kingdom". The new Prince's army did not hesitate, and the motley band enjoyed the blood-stirring experience unleashed by years of frustration and fear.

On they went, to attack the English-dominated settlements in North-West Wales at Denbigh, Flint, Hawarden and Holt. On 22nd September, they arrived at Oswestry, where the fires caused severe damage and people were forced to flee from their devastated homes, leaving behind their valuables for the wild Welsh army. Sweeping onwards without opposition, the rebels arrived at Welshpool (Y Trallwng).

News of their swift progress had already alerted Hugh Burnell of Shrewsbury to the immediate danger. He had time to levy men from the bordering districts of Shropshire, Warwickshire and Staffordshire. They were despatched to meet Glyn Dwr's rampaging Welshmen. On 24th September these well-trained soldiers halted the erratic march of the rebels, forcing them to disband and seek safety in the woods and mountains. Some of the Welsh scuttled back to their homes, as if nothing had happened. They had probably enjoyed a few days of burning and looting, but when it seemed that Glyn Dwr would soon be captured and killed, their patriotic fervour melted away like the morning mist. The English Marcher Lords were feared, and the peasants of those areas closest to the border probably felt that they had better lie low after a brief, but profitable, excursion. They had enjoyed the thrill and excitement of a quick raid, but fighting trained soldiers was not to be undertaken lightly. Back to their homes they went, secure in the knowledge that they would not be discovered in those days of anonymity. One peasant looked very like another.

King Henry marched south with all speed, the expert leader of forced marches, passing through Northampton, Coventry and Lichfield to reach Shrewsbury on 26th September. The danger of an attack on his border towns was over. The rebels had flown. It seemed that the English had once again asserted their supremacy without much exertion, yet this rising of Glyn Dwr's Welshmen had enflamed others in North Wales who saw the chance to stir up trouble in their own districts. The rebellion had begun.

It is customary in warfare to warn by example. The execution of one man in a village will often be sufficient deterrent, a necessary act to prevent further thoughts of disloyalty in the minds of others. At Shrewsbury, Henry ordered the death of Gronw ap Tudur, a Welshman of some importance locally who had been captured and accused of involvement with Glyn Dwr. According to medieval practice, his body was quartered, and the mutilated parts of his anatomy were placed on public display at Chester, Hereford, Ludlow and Bristol. This barbarous, effective justice was a warning to prospective traitors. How many travellers passing through the city gates must have raised their eyes to stare in fascinated horror at severed limbs. Such gory decorations would have caused many pangs of burgeoning patriotism to wither in the first rays of sunlight.

Early in the following month Henry led an army into the most troublesome area, following an uprising in Anglesey, travelling through Bangor and Caernarfon. Opposition there was led by Rhys Ddu, the Black, who attacked Henry's troops near Beaumaris. In retaliation, the English burned and plundered the house of Franciscan friars at Llanfaes Abbey, near Beaumaris, fully aware that the Franciscans were sympathisers with the Welsh hopes for freedom. This order of friars rejected personal possessions and followed the teaching of St Francis, a humble and gentle man who taught that love and humanity were more godly than ambition and wealth. The concept was unusual at a time when some churchmen were the wealthiest and most powerful, politically, in the country. The destruction of Llanfaes may seem unpardonable, but the English soldiers would have seen the valuables of a treacherous religious order as the booty of war; while the friars themselves owned nothing, their Abbey was rich and contained articles of great beauty and worth. Any of the men who had been with Henry to

Scotland would not have received much reward for their endeavours, and this was an opportunity to make some profit; looting always helped the captains to pay their men, and it was good for morale.

Another Rhys and his brother William, the sons of Tudor ap Gronw,* were cousins of Glyn Dwr who came from Anglesey. Tudor's wife Margaret, the sister of Helen, Glyn Dwr's mother, had married this descendant of an eminent Welsh family after her first union with William of Mawddwy. The family was to play an important role in the history of English kings. The two brothers may have decided to fight Henry for their own reasons, but their activities added to the upheaval. At this time, the new Prince was in hiding after the defeat of his forces on the banks of the Vrynwy at Y Trallwng in September. In angry mood, Henry would have assumed that all Welsh rebels were followers of Glyn Dwr, and the belligerent cousins were hunted as traitors whether their intervention was for personal glory or otherwise. The news, true or false, that there was armed support for Glyn Dwr in the Anglesey region would have travelled quickly through Snowdonia, and many must have believed that the Welsh rising was bigger than it actually was. Men believe what they want to believe.

The huge professional army of the King travelled through Wales, south from Bangor, tramping the rough tracks of Gwynedd to reach Mawddwy on 13th October and the comforts of Shrewsbury on the 15th. Along the route, Welshmen denied all knowledge of a rebellion, and sought Henry's protection from their rowdy countrymen. The abbotts of Bardsey and Cymmer rushed to swear their allegiance, along with many whose property was at risk. Doubtless they feared that the wild followers of Glyn Dwr might appropriate some of their abundant riches to help the Cause, and anyway, they enjoyed the peaceful life even if they were under an English thumb. The thriving Cistercian Abbeys owned vast estates which brought in considerable incomes; rebellions were bad for business.

The leaders of the rebellion remained at large as Henry returned to England after subduing the small disturbances in North Wales. Those who had been involved in the Carrog Conspiracy lost their lands, which were declared forfeit to the

*Tudor ap Gronw was a member of the Anglesey family of Ednyfed Fychan, ancestor of the Tudor dynasty.

Crown. Glyn Dwr's own manors, rents and revenucs were granted to John Beaufort, the Earl of Somerset, on 8th November, 1400. The Beauforts were rising rapidly in the wake of their half-brother's promotion. The estates of Gruffydd and Philip Hanmer were given to John Hanmer who had not helped his brother-in-law at this time.

Glyn Dwr's brother Tudor with the Dean of St Asaph and the seer bard Scab surrendered themselves to the King's mercy. Obviously the Scab had failed to prophesy such an early defeat for his Prince and protector. It appeared that the Cause was lost before it had begun, and the English Parliament congratulated itself on the speedy conclusion of this trivial matter. After the fierce Scots, the Welsh had been easy opponents. The soldiers of Henry's army were paid conscripts, accustomed to disciplined fighting and long marches. They were armed by their protectors, their lords, who were committed to feed and clothe them. The men-at-arms wore polished steel armour and carried an assortment of weapons such as the battle-axe and mace for close combat. English bowmen were feared throughout Europe; their wicked accuracy had slaughtered the French at Crecy. A skilled archer could kill a man at almost two hundred metres, firing twelve arrows a minute if the occasion demanded. A mere glimpse of such an imposing array was sufficient to make even the most courageous rebel retire to the hills and reconsider.

Glyn Dwr's followers were mostly peasants who went to war with a cloak and a snatched weapon. The more sophisticated leaders were not united, with Glyn Dwr's own brother skulking back to his manor to save his property and beg forgiveness from the King. Attacks had been disconnected and unplanned. In two months, Henry had won.

CHAPTER EIGHT

Smouldering Fires

"Deluded Pagans, fly with speed;
See, your bravest warriors bleed;
Through your thickest ranks his arm
Terror spreads and wild alarm."

Caesar Morgan.

EARLY in 1401, land-owners in the Border counties expressed fears in Parliament that their Welsh neighbours were not behaving like loyal subjects of the Crown. Nationalistic feelings had been aroused by the September rebellion the previous year which could not be ignored, even though Henry had acted with political clemency and granted pardons to all those who had answered Glyn Dwr's call. Although many Welshmen had hastily denied all thoughts of patriotism when faced with a direct choice, and Henry's soldiers, there were others who barely concealed their dislike of the English. Glyn Dwr and his friends must have had many sympathisers to hide them during these months, and they used the time to persuade relatives and friends that their desire for a free country was not an abortive spasm but a burning mission. It was noted that young Welsh scholars were leaving Oxford and other universities, making their way to the homeland as if alerted to the coming struggle. The Cause would have appealed to these exuberant students, particularly under a leader such as Glyn Dwr, and students are often the first to rally to a cause. Many Welsh labourers slipped back across the border, prepared to join the secret army. The call of the Cymry was strong.

The Government decided that strict legislative measures were necessary to protect their English citizens. These new laws severely limited the privileges of Welshmen living in England and the Marches. Welsh felons were to be executed immediately. Englishmen were to be protected from the "malice" of Welsh juries. The barons of the Marches were instructed to equip and garrison their castles. Yet this was not enough. Further laws were passed to ensure that the Welsh would have no chance of equality with their English counterparts. These laws, not unnaturally, caused resentment, and only served to fan the flames of a growing feeling that Wales must shake off the stifling rule of England — or exist as a vassal-state of Henry Bolingbroke. The legislation which had been intended to crush Welsh ambition achieved what Glyn Dwr's rebels could not; the blatant prejudice of the anti-Welsh laws provided the fuel which renewed the struggle.

The King's young son, Henry, was in command of the King's forces in North Wales operating from his base at Chester. Although still in his early teens, young Hal was already showing some of the steel that was to place him among the greatest of English military sovereigns. He was tall, strong, and an exceptional athlete. Hal was described by chroniclers as a handsome, well-proportioned youth whose love of hunting and knightly pursuits had resulted in a physical ability and agility far superior to the accomplishments of any of his fellows. The contemporary portrait of Henry V when he became king reveals the strength of character in his fine features which won so many followers, and such faith and loyalty that his name has been synonymous with the pride and courage of the English soldier since Agincourt. Placed in a position of authority at such an early age, Hal matured quickly.

His friend and companion in arms was Henry Percy, Hotspur, of Northumberland. Hotspur's abilities as a soldier had won him wide acclaim. His family's assistance to Bolingbroke had been rewarded by high office in the new regime. At this time, Hotspur was Justice of Chester, of North Wales, Sheriff of Flint, holder of Anglesey and Beaumaris, and Keeper of the lordship of Denbigh. While Shakespeare's Hotspur was a rough-mannered, blunt soldier with very little finesse, Henry Percy's strategy in the spring of 1401 was more diplomatic than military. Very craftily he offered pardons to those rebels who wished to surrender, excluding their leaders who could expect the same treatment as Gronw ap Tudor had received at Shrewsbury. The fickle followers of William and Rhys ap Tudor of Anglesey, grabbing the chance to return to a more peaceful life, in one piece, began to give themselves up to Hotspur and the English Prince, quickly forsaking their more stubborn countrymen.

William and Rhys, still in command of a small force, attacked Conwy on Good Friday of that year, which happened to be 1st April, while the devout populace of the town and the English garrison of the castle attended church. The great castle at Conwy was designed by Edward I's expert builder, James of St George, in the last decades of the thirteenth century. Impressively beautiful, and functional, it required very few men to maintain security. Conwy was part of Edward's master-plan to restore everlasting peace to North Wales, a peace enforced by the English. It formed part of the circle of castles which surround the natural fortress of Snowdonia, guarding the mainland from possible attack from the sea, from Anglesey and the western approach from Ireland. There were two entrances, although the smaller gateway was approached only by means of steps cut into the rock-face above the river. The main entrance was by a ramp and drawbridge, with more defences within the barbican to protect the interior. Richard II had sought the safety of Conwy, only to be lured out by the false assurances of Northumberland. Conwy Castle stands today, still magnificent, because it was such a superb stronghold that no army could ever force a way in. The walls are fifteen feet thick in places, to withstand the most severe bombardment; there are eight round towers to shelter observers from every possible angle of attack. Even the staircases were designed to hamper intruders, and to assist the defenders; nothing had been left to chance. Its situation on a steep-sided rock, bordered by rivers, made it virtually impossible for an enemy to use heavy siege-machines to any effect. Conwy was impregnable.

The two Tudor brothers used, instead, their native guile. Disguised as a carpenter, one of their supporters entered the castle quite openly, as maintenance and repairs were a continual process. As soon as the garrison went off dutifully to church, the carpenter overpowered the remaining warders and opened up the gate to William and his exultant band of rebels. Another small group led by Rhys remained in the surrounding hills to watch developments. Edward's impregnable fortress was now held by the Welsh, and the English soldiers found themselves locked out. They knew only too well that they were powerless and were forced to withdraw amid the mocking, jubilant catcalls of the new residents.

The humiliation and fury felt by Hotspur, who was directly

responsible to the King, must have been terrible. He made a futile attempt to attack the unflinching walls but was compelled to withdraw. Where siege-engines and cannons failed, starvation won. Supplies within the fortress did not last long, and the Welsh trouble-makers inside received no help from the townspeople of Conwy who were largely loyal to the English. It was, like most castle-towns in North Wales, a borough on the lines of English settlements with many immigrant merchant families who would not wish to incur the King's displeasure by helping traitors. They had no wish to damage their businesses or to suffer any personal depredations.

On 2nd May, at the nearby town of Caernarfon, Hotspur, as Justice of North Wales, held court sessions to receive protestations of loyalty from the people of Caernarfonshire and Merionethshire. These courts decided the level of dues they owed their King. At about this time, from inside the castle, came proposals for surrender from the starving inmates, which were eventually accepted, at the end of June. It was not until then, or early in July, that the prize was relinquished. The medieval rules of siege warfare allowed for negotiations which preserved honour on both sides when a stalemate had been reached.

Bold as the venture had been, it is not to the credit of the brothers that they obtained their freedom by surrendering some of their own men to Hotspur's mercy, while they themselves escaped. The hostages, chosen at random by William and Rhys, were summarily executed by Hotspur's soldiers as a warning to others, while a pardon was granted to the leaders, much to the annoyance of King Henry when the news reached him.

Hotspur's presence in the two counties ensured that the inhabitants there did not attempt any resistance to English forces, and as the gentry of Carnarfonshire and Merionethshire had sworn loyalty to the King, peace seemed assured. The Percy was responsible for maintaining peace by supplying men and equipment; he was obliged to pay for the campaign himself. It was expensive defending one's King, and Hotspur registered some complaints in a letter on 17th May. The ignominy of the episode was galling enough but the cost of the operation added considerably to the prickly Northerner's dissatisfaction.

On 30th May, Hotspur led English troops south as far as the

Mawddach and the Cader Idris range of mountains which tower over the small town of Dolgellau. An indecisive engagement was fought just outside the town with the result that the rebels fled to their mountain hideouts and Hotspur returned in frustration to Denbigh. His forces were still besieging Conwy at this time while the terms of surrender were being considered, and the maintenance of an army was costing a great deal of money. No doubt Hotspur expected payment to be sent to Denbigh in response to his request, but he waited in vain. Leaving affairs in Wales to subordinates, an angry commander returned to his family in Northumberland.

The Percies had provided men for Henry's army when he arrived at Ravenspur; they had sent troops to help Henry against the Scots and they had dutifully maintained their quota in Wales. Hotspur's anger and resentment were understandable. When the King later grumbled at the lenient treatment meted out to the rebel leaders at Conwy, a humiliation that was Hotspur's fault in the first place he added petulantly, young Percy must have reacted with suitable invective and barbaric fury within the privacy of his Northumberland home. A quick solution at Conwy had saved him further expense which was his prime consideration. The church-going Constable of Conwy, a Cheshire magnate John Massey, was pardoned on 2nd July, a gesture on Henry's part which may indicate that blame was not attached to Hotspur's mismanagement.

Perhaps the story is true that there was a meeting, or some communication, between Hotspur and Glyn Dwr during the summer of 1401. An amicable agreement or truce would have been extremely advantageous for Hotspur as it would have restored some of his lost prestige after the shambles of Conwy. Glyn Dwr was not yet fully committed, and the pardon granted to his cousins might well have been extended to include him at this time, if a powerful soldier such as Hotspur proposed it. But there was no sudden peace.

Throughout the early months of summer, the Welsh harassed targets chosen at random, and the sequence of events is not clear. Whether the rebels fought as independent units, as opportunists taking advantage of the turbulent times, or as parts of a co-ordinated army is not apparent. The hated English were attacked repeatedly, and those Welsh who were openly unsympathetic to the Cause were also the victims of looting and burning. Under the protection of the Marcher Lords, or peacefully going about their business in the rural districts around small castles, the inhabitants of central Wales were unprepared for the disruption. Property was destroyed; livestock was stolen; food was appropriated by the bands of insurgents for their own use.

There was a successful attack on the castle of New Radnor near Llandrindod Wells where some of the garrison were executed to dissuade others from thoughts of resistance. The Abbey of Cwm Hir in Radnor was ransacked and burnt. Cistercian monks were not friendly to the Welsh patriots; they had been very quick to profess their loyalty to King Henry although their motives may have been more pecuniary than holy. As Henry had devastated the Franciscan Abbey at Llanfaes to punish the minorite friars for suspected disloyalty to the crown, perhaps Glyn Dwr was demonstrating his own anger at disloyalty to the Welsh "Crown" with this vicious act of revenge.

The little town of Montgomery was ravaged and burnt. Success, with no real opposition, propelled the victors towards Y Trallwng, the scene of Glyn Dwr's first setback, to redress the balance. The Red Castle of Powys, or, as it is known, the Castle of Pole, guarded the Marches at Y Trallwng. The guardian, John Charlton, had been quick to raise levies of troops from the surrounding district to protect the valuable lands around Y Trallwng on the Shropshire-Welsh border where the tenants were wholeheartedly loyal to the King.

Glyn Dwr's forces withdrew from such an open engagement against the disciplined soldiers of Lord Charlton, though not before they had caused some material damage to the outskirts of the town. Their unco-ordinated and wild attack was a failure, and the Welsh prudently retreated to the mountainous districts a few miles away. It was easy for the rebels to split up, following the indistinct tracks which led along the upland contours to the safety of ancient hill-forts which still guard the territories of forgotten ancestors. From hidden eyries they could watch the progress of their hunters. When the English gave up the search the Welsh re-grouped and made new plans.

Reports of a great victory by the rebels at the River Hyddgen, in Powys, boosted morale, and fresh patriots arrived to support the Welsh forces as they planned to turn their steps towards the south west and Caerfyrddin (Carmarthen).

In the heart of Mid Wales lies the Plynlimon range of mountains. High in these hills, separated from the Cader Idris mass by the Dovey Valley, Glyn Dwr and his men must have sought shelter, secure within natural encampments just as the early inhabitants of Wales had protected themselves from invaders a millennium before.

It is likely that the militant actions of Prince Glyn Dwr had now begun to attract the services of more experienced soldiers. The Welsh archers who had served Richard II were expert fighters, with light, deadly weapons which gave them enviable mobility. Bowmen did not wear cumbersome armour but were dressed in leather jerkins which gave sufficient protection when attacking from a distance. The long bows of supple yew fired steel-tipped arrows which were aimed with deadly accuracy. There must have been many redundant Ricardian archers who welcomed the chance to fight again, especially under a Welsh Prince who was Henry's outlawed enemy. There were still rumours that Richard lived, and many to pretend that Glyn Dwr was fighting for the deposed King's return. It was a useful myth. Among the recruits were many Merioneth spearmen whose ferocity was legendary; they fought as their ancestors had fought, not bound by the codes of chivalry but driven by the more primitive urges of blood-lust and vengeance.

There were grand tales that Glyn Dwr intended to attack England, to subdue the hated English people and to stamp out the English language which had usurped the British tongue. It is doubtful that he ever considered such an ambitious course, since he was well aware of the strength of English forces. No doubt the rumours helped recruitment, and Glyn Dwr certainly hoped to drive the English out of his native Wales and to restore the Welsh language to its proper place as the accepted tongue of a free people.

And not only the English squatters were to be evicted. A large colony of Flemings lived in the area of western Pembrokeshire and that part of southern Cardiganshire which are both now in Dyfed, and on the Gower Peninsula near Swansea (Abertawe), which is now West Glamorgan. They had been granted land and were invited to settle in Wales by Henry I. Encouraged to continue their traditional crafts, the Flemings brought trade and prosperity to that rural part of England's western kingdom; but they also over-ran the native Welsh and ousted the Welsh language. The large force which attacked

(xiii) Battlefield Church near Shrewsbury.

(xiv) Hotspur's base at Denbigh Castle.

(xv) Llanelltyd Bridge near Dolgellau.

(xvi) A snow-covered pass near Cader Idris in May.

(xvii) Parliament House, Machynlleth.

(xviii) The Battle of Pilleth was fought on the hillside behind the Church.

(xix) Criccieth Castle.

(xx) The Castle of Laugharne held by Lord Carew.

(xxi) Harlech Castle guarding the coast of Ardudwy.

(xxii) Llyn Tegid, Bala Lake.

(xxiii) Gateway to Grosmont Castle.

(xxiv) Looking down at the Great Hall, Harlech Castle.

Glyn Dwr at Hyddgen, near what is now the Nant y Moch Reservoir to the east of Aberystwyth, was composed largely of Flemings who had no wish to lose their prosperous lands to some upstart traitor. Their unimaginative tactics proved no match for the mountain-based rebels, and reports that five hundred Welsh had defeated fifteen hundred well-armed attackers guaranteed a rise in Glyn Dwr's popularity among his hesitant countrymen.

At the end of May Henry ordered a muster of men drawn from fourteen counties. They gathered at Worcester, but once again Glyn Dwr and his men disappeared into the wild country, gathering more supporters as they traversed South Wales. They were at liberty to do as they pleased while Henry's army remained at Worcester.

For some reason, by the 8th June, the King was convinced that there was no immediate danger and that the trivial uprising had been merely an irritating convulsion which could be dealt with by local Marcher Lords. Lord Charlton's victory and repulse of the Welsh must have been reported to Henry at Worcester, news which would have lulled him into a false sense of security.

Between the last weeks of June and the beginning of September, there was nothing to prevent Glyn Dwr from consolidating his position by convincing his countrymen, by threat or persuasion, that his "rebellion" was justified. While his men made their presence felt by roaming the countryside, it seems likely that Owen hoped to attract much-needed allies to assist him as military leaders, and to give financial aid, from among the Welsh gentry who were not exactly rushing to his side. For the unemployed ex-soldier, or feudal peasant, the decision was a clear-cut choice between black Henry and the white hope of Wales. For the established landowner, perhaps with English connections, there was the distinct possibility that his wealth was at stake, as well as his life. Had not Owen's estates been confiscated? The man had been declared an outlaw and a traitor, and he faced certain death.

While the King made no move to march his Worcester army into Wales, inaction which may simply have been the result of financial problems, Glyn Dwr enlisted the help of many influential compatriots. By September the numbers of his supporters had risen considerably, and there was more than a little panic along the border. The threat of a Welsh invasion into England had become a dreadful possibility in the minds of worried citizens who lived in the more vulnerable townships and rich Abbeys of the Marches.

In response to the entreaties of these good citizens, and the news that Glyn Dwr was gathering some support from the people of South Wales, the King invaded his recalcitant dominion in October. His harsh treatment of Glyn Dwr's sympathisers was an obvious attempt to frighten people into betraying their Prince of the Cymry. Children were snatched as hostages; their parents were executed or disinherited if they had supported the traitor. On 9th October, Llywelyn ap Gruffydd Fychan was executed and quartered in the presence of the King at Llandovery (Llanymddyfri). This defiant squire had sons who were fighting for the Cause, but Henry's savage treatment of the prisoner was the result of Llywelyn's attempt at trickery. Apparently he had led the royal army round the countryside, supposedly guiding them to Glyn Dwr's hideout. These delaying tactics enabled the rebels to escape and Henry was made to look a fool. Accompanying him were Prince Henry and many other nobles who would not have taken kindly to Welsh trickery. It was necessary to make an example of the unrepentant squire.

The Cistercian Abbey of Strata Florida at Pontrhydfendigaid in Cardiganshire was plundered by the English army, yet another vicious act against a religious house, the defenceless prey of all invaders. Troops camped in the church right up to the high altar ignoring the sanctity of their temporary barracks. This time the reason was not the treachery or disloyalty of the friars, but because Strata Florida represented Welshness. The cemetery in the grounds contained the bones of former Welsh Princes, a place of sanctuary which aroused Henry's wrath. His soldiers were given free rein on this hallowed ground.

Many lands were confiscated and redistributed, as Henry punished those whose allegiance was suspect. The records reveal how much support there was for the rebel among the land-owners of Ystrad Tywi, the Vale of the River Tywi in the region of Llanymddyfri and Llandeilo (Dyfed). It is also true to say that there were many prepared to betray their more nationalistic neighbours, and a word in the right quarter enabled them to acquire discredited neighbours' estates. One of these beneficiaries was a Welsh gentleman, loyal to King Henry, called Dafydd Gam whose name occurs again at a later date as Glyn Dwr's hostage. Just as some made their fortunes by betrayal, there were others, more honourable and often from more humble backgrounds, who died rather than forsake their gallant leader. Their courageous silence meant that Henry never even glimpsed his adversary, nor knew of the secret hiding-places. For a month the English strode about Cardiganshire in frustration, constantly harried by unseen archers who picked off stragglers and jangled the nerves of weary soldiers from the safety of their hidden perches.

This was to be a new type of warfare, unlike the pitched battles that Henry had fought and won. The Welsh developed guerilla tactics, used successfully by their ancestors against other invaders, and by their kinsmen the Irish, which were to prove highly effective. No doubt many of the Welsh were unskilled in armed combat, lacking the training and fine weapons of the English. The numbers of bowmen were small, and the Merionethshire spearmen were more accustomed to hurling themselves at the enemy like a pack of wild wolves. It was their knowledge of the terrain, the country itself, and their ferocious belief in the Cause, that led to victory over superior forces. Yet Glyn Dwr did not have the support he so desperately needed.

Henry's cruel retribution, sound political strategy, had forced many to hesitate, or to condemn openly the insurrection of the Welsh Prince. Unable to discover Glyn Dwr, or to force a confrontation with the Welsh, the King returned to England leaving Hotspur's uncle, the Earl of Worcester, as Royal Lieutenant in South Wales. All the important garrisons were strengthened, from Aberystwyth to Llanfair-ym-Muallt and Llanymddyfri. It seemed as if the South had succumbed and Glyn Dwr was forced back to his original retreat in the North. Yet outside the protective walls of castles and fortified towns, no Englishman was safe.

Later in October the Welsh had re-grouped to attach Y Trallwng, the main base of the Charltons of Powys, no doubt in retaliation for the earlier defeat. A new Lord Charlton, Edward, had succeeded his recently deceased brother John, One report maintains that Prince Henry had been busily occupied in North Wales, leading his men around Snowdonia to drive any rebels south towards the King's forces. Hotspur, the formidable guardian of England's northern Marches, had departed on a mission to Scotland. In the absence of the veteran, the King's teenage son must have welcomed the opportunity to win himself a little glory. But his excursions gave the rebels the opportunity to attack his retinue and train which provided them with rich booty. Back to the hills of Merionethshire and Caernarfonshire went the gleeful patriots, where once again they had the support of the local inhabitants free from Hotspur's domination. They did not fear the boy-soldier on his first real campaign.

On the 2nd November, Glyn Dwr's forces attacked the castle of Caernarfon. The attempt failed and they sustained heavy losses; the great fortress had been built to withstand greater armies. The castle was held by a small garrison under the leadership of John Bold and as they had recently received their wages, and new provisions, they were in good heart. Obviously the soldiers had been cheered by the best encouragement for loyalty, adequate payment, and like Conwy, the stronghold was virtually impregnable. A frontal attack was utterly futile, but the rebels were now fired by patriotism and did not hesitate to try their strength, holding aloft their new standard, a golden dragon on a white field.

King Henry was finding the whole affair rather tiresome, and very expensive. Although he had won the throne, and begun his own reign by rebellion, Henry sought peace throughout his kingdom. There was little rest for the monarch as he dashed between Scotland and Wales, and faced unrest in Ireland along with the possibility of war against France. His nobles were also grumbling at the continual drain on their resources. Troops cost money, and while men were fighting they were not working. Each lordship was responsible for the upkeep of his levied forces and castles which had to be supplied and fitted out. When the King obtained funds from Parliament he could repay his nobles, but until then the burden fell on individuals. The Treasury was not open-handed, and great deliberations preceded each decision to reimburse the King. One of Henry's benefactors was the merchant Richard Whittington, whose generosity ensured that the King was at least able to dress the part. From Wales, the Prince sent many letters begging for funds, many of which were not regarded. The owners of privately-held castles were instructed to ensure their own safety, at their own expense.

Although he was undoubtedly a formidable soldier and an intelligent tactician, Henry was not imaginative. Unable to force Glyn Dwr into the open, the King must have thought that the Welsh leader was no real threat. All reports indicated that the Welsh fighters fled at the first signs of real opposition. Henry had fought in several battles where men stood their ground to be hacked down on the spot, or to emerge triumphant from a pile of dead foes. There were set rules for battles, and Glyn Dwr was not obeying the rules. He and his men were simply darting in and out of their mountain-lairs like a swarm of angry wasps, inflicting sharp stings but vanishing before many could be squashed. By strengthening his garrisons at strategic points, the castles which former English Kings had conveniently placed throughout Wales, Henry felt that the revolt would soon die out. As yet there was no real problem in South Wales, so the King concentrated on Mid Wales and the North. The South was put on the alert. Llanfair-ym-Muallt, Llanymddyfri, Caerfyrddin, Aberhonddu, Aberteifi, Aberystwyth and all major strongholds were in a state of readiness, garrisoned and supplied. Caernarfon had just proved its military strength; Conwy was again secure. The remaining fortresses of North Wales, including Harlech and Criccieth, were all safe and held by English loyalists.

Out of political clemency, Henry once again offered pardons to all those who would voluntarily surrender and renounce Glyn Dwr. Some accepted. In Cardiganshire, where the English army had destroyed whole areas of productive farmland and ransacked fine houses, the people must have reacted with some cynicism. They were also allowed, by royal decree and generosity, the privilege of speaking Welsh, an understanding gesture from the English King. It would have been difficult for a high proportion of the inhabitants to speak any other language. Henry's leniency may not have been as well received as he intended.

Towards the end of 1401, Glyn Dwr could have attempted a peace with the English. He had reason to think that the Northumberlands would support an amicable settlement if he had corresponded with Hotspur the previous summer. The Welshman's claim for the lands stolen by Lord Grey, the original thorn which had goaded him into action, was just and valid in law. The Percies had already grumbled about the expense of the continual military campaigns, and many other nobles must have felt similarly impoverished. The Earl of Northumberland had hoped for increased wealth by helping Henry to the throne, whereas the first two years of Bolingbroke's reign had cost him considerably more than he could hope to regain. The Percies may have mistrusted Lord Grey who had become a firm favourite at court. They would also have recognised that a valiant soldier such as Glyn Dwr, with all his followers, would be more use fighting for the English rather than as an outlawed rebel; Scotland was always a danger and they needed men to overcome the enemy in the North.

While his enthusiastic supporters had declared him Prince of Wales, Glyn Dwr himself had not apparently established a firm royal claim, or attempted to force the Welsh people to accept him as their Prince. At this time the majority preferred not to recognise him as the Welsh Saviour, or even as a compatriot, while the strength of England remained insuperable. Many were frightened; others were annoyed that these guerillas were upsetting peaceful relations with England. Prospects for a Welsh victory were not bright.

The Lord of Glyndyfrdwy could, perhaps, have been forgiven and forgotten if he had sought clemency. However, Henry was still influenced by Lord Grey, who preferred to have Glyn Dwr as an acknowledged traitor rather than as a difficult neighbour. With such an enemy close to the throne, Glyn Dwr could expect no mercy or forgiveness. The course of events raced past this opportunity for a peaceful settlement in Wales even if the leader had been prepared to sacrifice his own person.

As Henry could not maintain constant surveillance, Glyn Dwr had reclaimed his estates at Carrog and Cynllaith by force. Lord Grey had not taken up residence and the tenants were able to welcome their true lord back into their midst. His followers managed to survive the winter months by acquiring supplies whenever, and wherever, they could, and by hunting on the well-stocked lands of neighbouring barons. Towards the end of the year their leader decided that they were strong enough to continue the struggle and forfeited all possibility of reconciliation.

In December the Welsh launched an unsuccessful attack on Harlech Castle. Undaunted by their earlier failure at Caernarfon, they attempted to storm the walls of this square, squat fortress which could be approached by only one gateway. The attack was more of an aggravation than a serious exercise, and the arrival of English reinforcements from Chester caused a hasty withdrawal. The rebels continued their activities in the

Bangor area, where they looted and stole provisions before returning to their headquarters at Glyndyfrdwy to spend Christmas and the New Year. There they planned their future campaign, and enjoyed some of the more usual festivities in the comfortable surroundings of the Carrog manor.

The Welsh acquired a new confidence as they relaxed during the winter of 1401-2, preparing for further, more calculated resistance. Letters were sent abroad to persuade others to join the Welsh attack on England. Such requests between warring countries were not unusual in the Middle Ages. Quarrels between kings and princes often involved foreign monarchs who were called on to assist in struggles which were not directly their concern. A request written in Latin was sent to the Chiefs of Ireland. According to various predictions it had been foretold that the Irish and Welsh together would overcome the might of England. Possibly Glyn Dwr had met some of the Irish leaders during earlier campaigns with Richard II. The Irish would have been familiar with Lord Grey who had been a former Governor of Ireland and a sufficiently arrogant noble to inspire hatred. There was a great enmity between England and Ireland as the English had tried to steal lands by aggression and enforced peace by armed occupation.

These appeals for help, addressed to England's enemies, meant that Glyn Dwr had now no intention of seeking amnesty or of relinquishing the small victories he had won the previous year. All hopes of a pardon for the traitor were now destroyed. He was a threat to the English throne, and to the security of the whole country.

He wrote to Robert III of Scotland, asking for help as a kinsman and descendant of the same royal line. As the Scots were willing to snatch every opportunity of upsetting their neighbours the northern kingdom did open negotiations; there was a possibility of help from that direction. Owen's claim of kinship was extremely tenuous and may have been more imaginary than factual, but it was not beyond the bounds of credibility and the assertion was not challenged.

If the Adam of Usk letters which survived are genuinely Owen's compositions, or even close copies of originals, they reveal something of Glyn Dwr's personality and education which is valuable when so little is known definitely of his character, of the man himself. The letter to Scotland's king was written in

French. There were close links between France and Scotland, and both countries were England's perennial foes. French had been the common language of all three countries among the nobility for centuries, so it was natural that the Welsh Prince, educated alongside the sons of aristocrats, should use the chivalric tongue of the upper classes. The new English language was just acquiring a foothold, and although contemporary literature was speeding its development, it was still the vernacular of peasants and tradespeople.

Variations in vocabulary and spelling made written English a difficult medium to understand, especially by a foreigner; French was the natural choice for correspondence between kings. Glyn Dwr's native Welsh was not comprehensible to anyone outside Wales.

In both letters Owen refers to the enemy as "Saxons", appealing to both the more ancient, indigenous British races to unite with their brothers, the Celts in Wales, against this hated race of invaders. It is interesting that the Saxons are the object of his hatred, rather than the more recent Normans. Glyn Dwr goes into great detail and quotes a list of royal antecedents dating back to the days immediately after the Roman occupation when Britons controlled Britain. Wave after wave of Saxons, or English, had forced the Britons to retreat, and it was the invading race of English who had given the Britons the name, Welsh, meaning ironically, Foreigners. The Welsh from Cumbria, or Cumberland, had become known as the Cymry, or Comrades, and they had taken control of North Wales early in the seventh century. This pre-occupation with events of earlier centuries is characteristic of the Welsh, even today. Eight hundred years had passed between the Saxon invasion and Glyn Dwr's uprising, yet he regarded the Saxons as the enemy. In the twentieth century it is not uncommon to see the slogan, "Remember 1282", a reminder that the Welsh hero Llywelyn fought the English in order to free Wales. This stark, enigmatic admonition has little meaning for passing tourists, but the people of Wales understand, and remember.

Glyn Dwr must have decided that the Irish "cousins" would be more easily persuaded by reference to prophecies than lineage, and he asks for help on the basis of an ancient tale. Irish and Welsh blood had been mixed for thousands of years as the result of trade between the two countries across the narrow Irish Sea. The early rulers of South Wales had come from Ireland, and the western coast of North Wales had been populated by Irish settlers. Welsh heroes of legend and folk-tale are inextricably mixed with the sons of Ireland.

Both letters request additional soldiers, indicating that his own forces were certainly not strong enough to withstand a concerted English attack. Both letters are carefully composed, by a clever hand, deferential and courteous but making the situation very clear; the writer is obviously convinced that right is on his side. Glyn Dwr's wide knowledge and sound education were considerable assets, and the requests show that he felt himself the equal of any other royal leader. The recipients must also have realised that Glyn Dwr was no barbarian; this Welsh Prince was worthy of their attention.

While he awaited results from these appeals, Glyn Dwr approached other Welshmen. It would have been expensive trying to feed and equip his forces from his own dwindling purse, and there was a limit to what they could steal. He had to provide food for the men, fodder for the animals, adequate shelter and more weapons. He needed help from men of his own class. Many were not courageous enough, or sufficiently Welsh, to take his side. Some members of his own family were not committed to the Cause, such as Hywel Sele of Nannau near Dolgellau. They preferred to remain loyal to the English crown rather than risk their lands, or lives, for a man who had lost his own fortune as a result of the rebellion. While the manors of Glyndyfrdwy and Sycharth were in the hands of the rebels, the rents and revenues were not. It was not inconceivable that Glyn Dwr would be evicted from his former estates as soon as the King had time to deal with the upstart Prince. Relatives of the family must have hoped that the business would soon be settled, without any recriminations against them.

The days of luxurious living, plentiful food and gorgeous clothing were fast disappearing. Glyn Dwr's support came from the people. Very slowly, he was gaining the confidence of more influential followers who would help him, but for the moment his troops were obliged to live as outlaws, stealing in order to exist, with more faith than proven ability. Glyn Dwr was totally committed to his belief in a Free Wales. The hardships would be worthwhile.

CHAPTER NINE

Great Omens

"At that time, throughout all England, a portent such as men had never seen before was seen in all the heavens."
Anglo-Saxon Chronicle.

THE Welsh Cause was fully supported by influential bards, who travelled the countryside relaying information, convincing the isolated communities that their Saviour had arisen. Poems and songs glorified the deeds of this mighty soldier who would free Wales from the crushing oppression of England. Scattered villages in North and Mid Wales would have heard little of events, other than rumour and conjecture. There was no means of verifying the news they did receive, and the bards doubtless conveyed information they wished to hear. Glyn Dwr's strength came from his appeal to ordinary people, peasant-labourers, tenant-farmers and hillmen of pure Welsh blood whose reactions were those of their ancestors. As Gerald of Wales had commented in the twelfth century, the Welsh were quick to answer the call to battle, rushing from their ploughs to pick up weapons.

There were other factors which, in the view of some historians, were the prime cause of the Welsh revolt. In the previous century, the Black Death had wiped out whole villages in England, causing a shortage of labour. The plague had affected the social structure of Britain as a whole, as workers had been able to demand higher wages and more freedom of movement. Although the peasants had not achieved unlimited freedom, villeinage was fast disappearing, and the landowners were compelled to pay higher wages or leave their lands uncultivated. In England, Wat Tyler had led an unsuccessful revolt against the high taxation imposed by Richard's ministers, but the revolutionary wave of discontent had continued unabated.

Welsh labourers had not been slow to seek work in England, where they could sell their services to the highest bidder. The reaction to these new circumstances had been less obvious in

Wales, but workers must have felt that here was an opportunity to escape some of the rents and taxes they were forced to pay their English landlords. Itinerant workers who returned to the homeland spread the disaffection. Now the Welsh had a chance to win a whole country, not just concessions. The new socialism, embodying the ideals of freedom, gave Glyn Dwr's movement the impetus it needed.

Early in the spring of 1402, an approaching comet lit the skies over North Wales. It was remarkable for its splendour, visible for several weeks, shedding its strange light over the wondering country-folk who could find but one explanation. It was still many years before anyone could offer a scientific explanation for astronomical spectaculars. Interest in the heavens was purely astrological; eclipses, comets and inexplicable lights were interpreted as messages from the Almighty, or from more ancient gods. They were either warnings of disaster, or they heralded great events, depending on the observer's viewpoint. The Bayeux Tapestry, commemorating the Battle of Hastings, shows Halley's comet glowing brightly as the conflict down below on earth decided England's future. The people who observed the dragon-shape of the 1402 comet knew of other mysterious stars. There had been one over Bethlehem; there had been one to herald the birth of Arthur, son of Uther Pendragon, seen by the magical Merlin. This third great star must surely herald the rise of their own Saviour, the Lord of Glyndyfrdwy, who would lead the men of Wales from their bondage to glorious freedom. We may imagine the interpretation of such an opportune manifestation in the mouths of the bards, whose learning and mystic powers enabled them to explain such phenomena. Perhaps Glyn Dwr himself felt that he was chosen for a special purpose, as Shakespeare's Glendower insists:

> *"The heavens were all on fire, the earth did tremble."*

While Owen's devoted follower, the bard Iolo Goch, made full use of the portent to convince his countrymen that the leader had indeed arrived, the English were similarly perturbed when the tail of the comet apparently pointed towards Wales, a dire warning of imminent danger from the west. It was a dragon in the sky, foretelling the dragon on earth.

Accompanying the comet were severe storms and exceptionally bad weather. Great winds swept the countryside that February of 1402 while the terrifying visitor blazed in the heavens on its journey across the firmament.

Fortified by this sign, the Welsh attacked the lordship of Ruthin to punish Lord Grey for his incessant spite against Glyn Dwr. They stole and plundered in Dyffryn Clwyd, the valley of Clwyd, but did not attack the neighbouring settlement at Denbigh. This restraint is significant, as Denbigh was held by the absent Hotspur, against whom Glyn Dwr did not bear such malice. Henry Percy was instructed to return to North Wales at the end of March, and orders were sent to the King's Chamberlain at Chester to prepare for an attack.

During April Lord Grey himself led a force to capture his detested enemy. His men were drawn from the lands of Dyffryn Clwyd, where loyalties were divided; the commander should have been more sensitive to the emotions of his levied troops. Betrayed by some of his own soldiers, Grey fell into an ambush, and Glyn Dwr's reputation soared. The capture of the Marcher Lord of Ruthin was a signal to those who had hesitated, waiting to see which way the wind would blow. Men suddenly realised that this Welsh baron was more powerful than they had imagined, and converts rushed to join the Prince's army. Unhindered, the jubilant Welsh attacked St Asaph in the Vale of Clwyd, where they ravaged the cathedral and the bishop's palace. Bishop Trevor had been the first to warn King Henry of the danger that was developing in Wales after Glyn Dwr's petition had failed early in 1400. The Bishop had remained loyal to Henry, and suffered the consequences. Many of his personal possessions and the valuable contents of the Abbey, worth a considerable fortune, disappeared into the hills with the rebels, the legitimate booty of war.

Hotspur, recalled to duty, recognised the danger and organised a naval expedition to guard and supply the English castles along the North Wales coast. He went to superintend the mustered forces at Denbigh, and soon realised that circumstances had changed during his absence. A new feeling of unity, and enmity, had been aroused; the Welsh were rapidly increasing in strength. The merry month of May closed on an uneasy note for the English.

Glyn Dwr did not wait to be attacked by Hotspur. His strategy remained that of the guerilla leader, purposely avoiding the open battle of armour-clad knights on heavy horses.

Using hardy, sure-footed Welsh ponies the Welsh army disappeared into the mountains. They had fought in this manner for generations and saw no reason to change tactics. Lord Grey was imprisoned, held securely by merciless captors who knew his worth only too well.

In June Glyn Dwr travelled through part of Powys organising skirmishes from the safety of the uplands in Maelienydd, the Border lands owned by the House of Mortimer. Herefordshire was a beckoning target, with the prospect of good looting and easily-acquired food. The Welsh made swift sorties, choosing random targets, with increased confidence and daring.

On 22nd June, St Alban's Day, the Welsh finally stood their ground and won a great victory at Bryn Glas, a hillside near Pilleth where many brave knights were killed by the rebels. A large force had marched out to meet the raiders, led by Edmund Mortimer who was the brother of the Earl of March whose death in Ireland in 1398 had left young sons; now in Henry's custody. Edmund managed the estates on their behalf, and in their absence, since his nephew was legally the heir to the throne and Henry felt that it was wiser to keep the Mortimer youth under his protection. Reports indicate that the Welsh were led by Rhys Gethin, a highly competent but wild captain of the more temperate Glyn Dwr.

As the Mortimer men were levied from Hereford and the surrounding district, many of them were Welsh archers compelled to serve the Marcher Lord under duress. During the battle, which took place virtually on the border near Knighton (Trefelo-y-Clawdd) in the valley of the Lugg, the archers turned patriots and joined with their countrymen against Mortimer. Accounts give the numbers of dead at several thousands. The corpses were left on the hillside where, some writers have asserted, the Welsh camp-followers mutilated the remains in horrible fashion.

The crime was committed by women, many of whom possibly fought alongside their men although most would have been the traditional companions of armed forces, acting as cooks and comforters. Their barbarity is recorded by Shakespeare in the introductory scene of *Henry IV, Part One.* Their behaviour may be condemned, but similar atrocities have occurred in more recent times, notably during the French Revolution, and even during this century when the cruelty of men and women has reached new heights.

The Elizabethans were introduced to Owen Glendower by Westmoreland's graphic account of this Welsh victory:

> *"A thousand of his* [*Mortimer's*] *people butchered;*
> *Upon whose dead corpses there was much misuse,*
> *Such beastly shameless transformation*
> *By those Welshwomen done as may not be*
> *Without much shame retold or spoken of."*

Such a story, probably exaggerated, would have convinced the English that they were dealing with savage barbarians. It is reasonable to comment that Glyn Dwr's followers were difficult to control. Unlike their leaders they had not been educated or brought up with the rules of chivalry. A victory was a victory. It is maintained that the bones of the fallen were still being uncovered by the plough not too long ago, so many fine men were massacred that day.

Edmund Mortimer was taken prisoner, a fortuitous capture that gave Glyn Dwr two important hostages; Grey was still held. Among the captives was Thomas Clanvow, to whom has been ascribed the Chaucerian poem, "The Cuckoo and the Nightingale", although confusion among various authorities raises some doubts about this assertion.

When Henry heard of the disaster he summoned a general muster to meet at Lichfield in July, but England was again threatened by the Scots in the North. France was also contemplating hostile action, as Henry's accession to the throne had resulted in the deposition of Richard's Queen, the daughter of the King of France. Henry was undoubtedly "shaken and wan with care", and the planned invasion of Wales was temporarily abandoned as English troops moved north to face the greater danger, leaving Glyn Dwr free to consolidate his victory without fear of reprisal.

More supporters flocked to join the victor. Men were urged to go and fight the good fight by Franciscan monks who saw an opportunity to overthrow the usurper. They had always supported Richard, and now provided financial aid for their lost King's Champion. Glyn Dwr, very sensibly, did not dissuade them or point out that they were under some misapprehension. The myth that he was fighting for King Richard's honour and the restoration of the Plantagenet line was extremely useful. While Glyn Dwr's star was in the ascendant many who had safe-guarded their interests by supporting Henry now joined the Welsh guerillas who were apparently winning.

During August they marched through South Wales, ravaging Gwent, and Glamorgan (now split into West, Mid and South Glamorgan), hurling forces at the strongholds of Abergavenny, Usk, Caerleon, Casnewydd, and Caerdydd. They enjoyed such success that Henry was compelled to leave the Scottish campaign in the hands of the Northumberlands and march to Shrewsbury for consultation with his worried Marcher Lords. He placed his son, Henry of Monmouth, in command of a force at Chester; the Earl of Stafford led a force at Hereford, while he personally led a force into Wales determined to destroy the rebels and eradicate the source of irritation.

While the royal forces were chasing Rhys Gethin round the South, Glyn Dwr had withdrawn to the North. The two Anglesey brothers, William and Rhys Tudor, reappeared on the scene, leading a new group of spearmen into the fray. Apparently the Conwy affair had preserved only their fame, and the infamous surrender was tactfully forgotten, or disclaimed. Along the coast, the English castles of Harlech, Criccieth and Caernarfon were reminded that the Welsh campaign was serious. The uprising, like all civil upheavals, divided families. Along the coastal belt of Wales, where English immigrants had prospered and married into Welsh families, the division of loyalties was unavoidable. Brother found himself opposed to brother; cousin against cousin. Robert Meredith of Criccieth fought alongside Glyn Dwr, while his brother Ieuan was the co-defender of Caernarfon Castle at side of John Bold. The irreconcilable beliefs of English and Welsh caused much sorrow and bloodshed in Anglo-Welsh homes, and it was this fear of reprisal from one side or the other which led to so many instances of shifting loyalties when the occasion demanded.

In the South where the King planned to defeat Glyn Dwr's followers by a magnificent show of strength, it would have been folly to meet the King's army on equal terms, so the guerillas fought their own darting, devastating way, attacking quickly, retreating safely, attacking again. That September the weather was abominable, and Henry's men suffered miserably in the autumn storms, bogged down in mud, cold, wet and terrified of nocturnal raids. They were short of supplies as much of their food was lost or ruined in the torrential rain and hurricane-force winds. They could not replenish their stores from local sources as the harvest was destroyed; Rhys Gethin's men had already taken what was available. The English suffered from exposure as they lay, largely unprotected, night after night following equally dismal days, in the open countryside. Tents were blown down; horses bolted. Thunder and lightning tore the skies apart.

After a fortnight of unabated misery, the huge army was disbanded, either to seek shelter within the English castles in the area or to retreat over the border in complete disarray. It was a frustrating and dismal venture led by a wet and weary King. Welsh supporters gleefully attributed the bad weather to the magical arts of their leader and Henry must have felt that they might be right. Glyn Dwr, protected by supernatural powers, could use the elements as well as his archers to defeat the enemy.

A disgruntled King Henry must have been delighted at the news he then received from Scotland. The Northumberland Percies had achieved a great victory over the marauding Scots at Homildon Hill. When he heard that they had taken many important and rich hostages, Henry saw the Percies' prize as a providential windfall. His congratulatory message contained an accompanying command which was to affect the Welsh Cause considerably, although its importance could not have been envisaged, The Percies were instructed to hand over their valuable prisoners to the King, an utterly outrageous proposal which was without precedent and against all accepted custom. Henry seems to have acted quite contrary to his political nature, as any intelligent man could have anticipated the Northumberlands' reaction to such a demand. Yet the possibility that there would be a downright refusal cannot have occurred to hard-pressed Henry Bolingbroke as he desperately sought money from any source. He was the sovereign, and his subjects must obey.

As the English army had been unable to subdue rebellious Wales by force, England's Parliament introduced new laws to harass the obstinate Welsh. Recognising the influence of the bards, a law was passed to forbid "wastrels" from addressing any gathering. It became unlawful to meet at all, as all congregations were banned. Welshmen could not bear arms, nor hold residences capable of being defended. Supplies were restricted. No Welshman could hold public office, nor could anyone married to a Welsh woman. As well as causing domestic friction, this particular law would have aroused animosity among Glyn Dwr's own countrymen since not all Welshmen supported the Cause, yet they were to be penalised. The only exceptions, concerning public office and the defence of buildings, applied to churchmen who retained their positions and were at liberty to defend their property. Men of God were apparently above suspicion.

During November, negotiations were completed for the ransom of Lord Grey. His importance to the King was revealed by the "committee" authorised to make arrangements, consisting of five knights and six other high-ranking men. The ransom money was paid to Glyn Dwr, six thousand marks with a further four thousand marks pledged by Grey's son. This colossal amount meant new riches for the Welsh, but ruination for the Marcher Lord who died a poor man.

Mortimer was in a different position and could expect no swift intervention, or large ransom to procure his release. Henry was probably quite pleased that Edmund was held a prisoner, in danger of his life, at the whim of the barbaric Welsh.

Henry Bolingbroke was fully aware that the House of Mortimer had a more legitimate claim to the throne than his own family. When Roger Mortimer, the Earl of March, had been killed in Ireland during 1398, the heir to his extensive estates was his son Edmund, a boy of ten. As a lineal heir to the throne, the young Earl of March was regarded as a threat, and possible rallying-point for Richard's supporters. Richard had produced no heirs. Bolingbroke had taken the boy into his own family, where he grew up with the royal children, safely under the eye of Henry himself. By this action the King prevented any plot against the Lancaster family which might have evolved around the person of Edmund. There was one unsuccessful plot during Henry's first months as King, but the conspirators were betrayed. The assassination attempt served only to alert the King to the danger of allowing an heir to live, and although young Edmund was well-treated, he was a prisoner, under constant supervision. His claim was directly through his father, Roger, whose mother had been the daughter of the Duke of Clarence. Lionel's position had been senior to that of his brother, John of Gaunt. While both Lionel and John were sons of Edward III, the young Earl of March should have been King at Richard's death since Clarence was the older brother. The boy Edmund's descent through the female line was unquestionably legitimate.

No serious attempts were made to free the boy's uncle, Edmund Mortimer, and during his captivity he became personally involved with Glyn Dwr's family by marrying one of the chieftain's daughters. This was the musical Lady Mortimer of Shakespeare's play who spoke no English, but whose devotion to her Lord is expressed in the language of the Cymry. The House of Mortimer could also claim descent from Llywelyn the Great, through the marriage of Llywelyn's daughter, Gladys the Dark to Ralph Mortimer of Wigmore.

The alliance was beneficial to both sides. The rebel Welshman could offer his support to the Mortimer claim on the throne, and the Earl of March's formidable archers, under uncle Edmund's command, were of great advantage to the Welsh. By December Mortimer was re-established at Maelienydd, writing to the knights of Hereford to tell them of the new alliance, asking them for their support alongside the House of Mortimer against King Henry.

Henry's failure to ransom Mortimer brought another bonus. Edmund's sister was the wife of Henry Percy, the Hotspur of the North. Recognising that their King had not acted in their best interests, because he had been quite prepared to sacrifice Edmund to safeguard the throne, the House of Northumberland felt slighted. The King should have made every effort to free their brother-in-law, and his apathy obviously sprang from fear, or mistrust, of the Mortimers. By implication, he also felt no obligation to any Mortimer relation such as Henry Percy. It seems probable that there was correspondence between Edmund and his sister, Lady Percy. It is certain that the Percies decided that an alliance with Glyn Dwr, Prince of the Cymry, a man respected and admired by them, would offer a new opening for their ambitions. The Earl of Northumberland had been largely responsible for putting Henry on his throne; events of the past year caused him to entertain doubts concerning the usurper's intentions. A Welsh emissary, William Lloyd of Foxall, near Denbigh, travelled secretly to Berwick to make the necessary arrangements.

A new pattern was emerging. Henry, totally unaware of the Northumberland conspiracy, was anxious to quell the troublesome Welsh. His son, Henry, was proving to be an able soldier, which was fortunate for the harassed monarch. Troubles came from all directions, forcing the King to guard his northern borders while he sought to establish himself in the west. His army was continually divided, which enabled the Welsh rebels to roam at will through the Border counties and throughout Wales, without fear of retaliation on a large scale. They would appear, then disappear, like shadows. They attacked English castles and placed them under siege. Harlech and Aberystwyth were suffering badly, without supplies and with no sign of assistance. The remote garrisons were entirely cut off as it was dangerous for anyone to travel the countryside without armed protection. Glyn Dwr's men ensured that strangers could not approach, and he had sufficient followers now to maintain active hostilities throughout his "kingdom".

Glyn Dwr knew also that he had further help to come, both from Mortimer and his neighbours in Hereford, and from the great Percies. Henry IV had reason to be "shaken and wan with care" as the year of the comet drew to a close.

It was during 1402 that one of the many legends gained credence, a story that has preserved Glyn Dwr's name, and which reveals the enmity of those who did not support the Welsh Cause. Sir Walter Scott wrote in *Marmion:*

"All nations have their omens drear,
Their legends wild of love and fear;
Bethink him of Glyndowerdy,
And shun the spirit's Blasted Tree."

The Lord of Nannau, an estate near Dolgellau, was Hywel Sele, one of Glyn Dwr's cousins. He supported the Lancastrians, as did the monks of nearby Cymmer Abbey who asked for Henry's protection at the beginning of the uprising. Whether invited by the Cistercian abbott of Cymmer to arrange a truce, or as an unwelcome visitor trespassing on Nannau land, Glyn Dwr and a small force of men encountered Sele close to the family mansion. Some stories suggest that he had gone with the intention of persuading Sele to join him, or at least to close the unfriendly gap that had developed between the two cousins. Others report that the roving band had decided to help themselves to some of the game on the Nannau estates. As they were close to Harlech, which was under siege, it is possible that they were out hunting for fresh food for themselves to break the monotony of guarding the sea-side fortress.

Discovering the intruders, perhaps fearing that he would be accused of helping the rebels, Sele accosted them and tried to prevent his cousin from hunting on his land. He failed to kill Glyn Dwr, but was murdered by the Welsh leader, or his men. The legend tells us that Sele's body was hidden in an oak tree, and remained undiscovered until the trunk was split open by lightning many years afterwards. Sele's ghost was believed to haunt the area, which ensured that local people avoided the Haunted Oak, a tree that was destroyed, again by lightning, in the last century.

Other versions of the story tell how Glyn Dwr was an invited guest at Nannau, out hunting with his cousin when Sele turned to shoot an arrow directly at him. Saved by a vest of chainmail, Glyn Dwr killed Sele in self-defence, hiding the body in the tree. When Glyn Dwr lay dying he sent his friend Madoc to tell Sele's widow the grim secret, as she had mourned the inexplicable disappearance of her husband for ten years.

The first story goes on to tell that the rebels burned the mansion of Nannau, but were ambushed at Llanelltyd Bridge, near Cymmer Abbey, by Sele's son-in-law from Ganllwyd. After a fierce fight they escaped and fled to the security of Sycharth Castle, near Llansilin.

The present Georgian building, on the site of the old mansion, can be seen two miles along the Llanfachreth (Llanfachraeth) road from Dolgellau, overlooking lovely parkland. The Haunted Oak fell in 1813, and the sounds of a wandering soul were heard no more, while a monument to Hywel Sele was erected at Cymmer which now stands in ruins alongside Llanelltyd Bridge.

The legends must be based on some remnant of truth, but centuries have obscured the facts, other than the example of non-co-operation from people who could have been expected to support a fight for the freedom of their country.

CHAPTER TEN

Attacks and Retreats

"I am the Prince of Wales; and think not, Percy,
To share with me in glory any more;
Two stars keep not their motion in one sphere;
Nor can one England brook a double reign,
Of Harry Percy and the Prince of Wales."

William Shakespeare.
Henry IV, Part One.
Act V scene iv.

EARLY in 1403, young Prince Hal was not leading the riotous tavern-life of Shakespeare's character, but was inevitably transformed by events into Henry the Soldier. He was sixteen years old. From the earliest days of his childhood he had been trained for such a career and his undoubted inbred talent proved invaluable to the King. He was appointed Royal Deputy in Wales, in command of troops from the Border counties. Unlike his famous grandfather, John of Gaunt, the young Prince did not have to live in the shadow of older brothers. John had waited many years before he could prove his military skill and win fame on the field rather than admiration at the tournament.

Eager to establish himself at once, Henry of Monmouth proceeded to lead a vigorous attack on the rebel headquarters. During May the Prince's forces marched from Shrewsbury and destroyed Sycharth near Llansilin, Glyn Dwr's lovely home at Cynllaith. The surrounding estates were devastated, the buildings burnt to the ground. This delightful manor which had seen such gaiety and prosperity was reduced to a smouldering ruin.

The English Prince of Wales marched on to Carrog, in the Vale of Llangollen, where his men demolished the Prince of the Cymry's other home at Glyndyfrdwy. The lodge was utterly destroyed and the area in the immediate vicinity ravaged. Prisoners were executed as suspected sympathisers; innocent or guilty, no clemency was shown now. Whatever feelings this young soldier had entertained for Glyn Dwr previously, his attitude now was that of a royal Prince towards a traitor. The knowledge that Glyn Dwr had approached England's enemies for military aid, secrets which had been learned from the interception of letters, coupled with the dangerous Mortimer alliance, were factors to ensure that Henry of Monmouth concentrated on the elimination of this threat to the King and to himself as heir to the throne. Although Henry Bolingbroke had taken the throne by force, an illegal entry through the back door, Prince Henry would not lightly surrender his own beckoning future by allowing a paltry Welsh baron to demoralise a royal army. Confident, and full of enthusiasm, Prince Henry occupied northern Merioneth.

Once again Glyn Dwr was assisted by renewed activity in Scotland, where the King's attention was fully occupied. The Welsh rebels were able to continue their harassment of English-held castles at Conwy, Caernarfon, Rhuddlan and Criccieth. Both Harlech and Llanbadarn at Aberystwyth were besieged, and suffering so badly that Prince Henry wrote to his father in some desperation. He was anxious to press on into these coastal areas to relieve the starving and demoralised garrisons who were totally surrounded by hostile Welshmen. A letter was despatched to the King asking for more military support and more funds.

The companies who served the King were protected by contracts made by their captains. Expenses of transport and wages for the troops were met by the Exchequer, which was controlled by the Commons. Payments were often delayed, but this method ensured that essential equipment and supplies were provided to enable captains to pay wages to their soldiers, eventually.

The captains were professional soldiers, gentlemen by birth, who were retained by the sovereign and financed by grants of land or annuities so that there was a permanent reserve of fighting-men at the King's command. Each lord and knight was expected to provide troops, drawn mainly from retainers and tenants, so that any part of the kingdom could be mobilised at a moment's notice. Each captain had to stipulate the number of men-at-arms and archers he could muster, together with their equipment and horses. There were many men who had become professional soldiers, who were willing to enlist with any lord or knight, providing they received some reward. These mercenaries, mainly archers, formed the bulk of a king's army regardless of the enemy, and often enlisted with the same captain for subsequent campaigns. This method of raising troops explains how Henry was able to muster huge numbers of men, equipped and ready for action, at very short notice.

Captains, the lords and knights, were able to make a profit by selling important captives for ransoms and by acquiring booty after successful campaigns. The troops fighting in Wales were not likely to make much profit since there were few wealthy hostages to pay ransoms, and booty was poor, or non-existent. There was barely enough food in the non-productive areas of Snowdonia, except stray livestock and game which had to be hunted. Mercenaries who had fought in France, or even in Scotland, must have been very disgruntled. The few scattered monasteries, where items of real value could be found, were loyal to King Henry, so there was no excuse for ransacking the Cistercian houses. In addition, Glyn Dwr's men had already helped themselves as they were also in need of money, food and supplies. An abbott with any intelligence had long since removed his valuables to a safe place, trusting neither side.

Prince Henry's soldiers began to desert in large numbers, and he had difficulty persuading them to wait for their wages which were delayed by a grudging Exchequer. Before the beginning of July he did receive a thousand pounds from London, but no further help was sent to replace the diminished force or to replenish his supplies. The money barely covered what he already owed. Some extra men were levied along the border, but this was a defensive measure after news that Glyn Dwr intended to raid the rich countryside on the fringes of Wales. The young Prince could not, after all, lead his men to victory.

Typically, while Prince Henry was occupied in the North, and later languishing reluctantly at Shrewsbury, fretting with impatience at the slowness of the Exchequer, Glyn Dwr's forces were active in the South. He now had enough followers to spread his banner across the country. Sieges were maintained unremittingly around the northern strongholds, leaving the leader free to consolidate his position in South Wales.

One group of rebels attacked Aberhonddu Castle, which belonged to Henry himself through the inheritance of his first wife, Mary de Bohun. They were unsuccessful and had to retreat after suffering heavy losses. News of this reversal may have cheered King Henry, but by 2nd July Owen had appeared in person to put new heart into the Welsh rebels of the Tywi valley. They hurried to join him, swearing oaths of fealty to prove their newfound enthusiasm. Llanymddyfri was attacked with ferocity before the patriots moved westwards towards Dinefwr, an intimidating array of eight thousand lances causing unprecedented alarm among the formerly complacent castellans. On the 3rd July they camped at Llandeilo then marched on to Dryslwyn the following day, recruiting more men as they marched. The gates of Dryslwyn were thrown open by the warden, Rhys ap Gruffydd, and Glyn Dwr was welcomed into the castle.

The inhabitants of nearby Carreg Cennen were terrified; there were ladies trapped within the castle by this swift advance. The Keeper, John Scudamore, requested safe passage for the women, but his plea was ignored. Obviously Glyn Dwr's attitudes had hardened considerably over the past few years. The gentle, family man of the 1390's had become an unemotional crusader, driven by circumstances to forget his chivalrous upbringing. A century later, Macchiavelli was to write in *Il Principe,* Chapter XV:

> "(The Prince) will find that some of the things that appear to be virtues will, if he practices them, ruin him, and some of the things that appear to be wicked will bring him security and prosperity."

The cultured courtier had been compelled to adjust his thoughts, and actions, to the more ferocious methods of his compatriots. Similar transformations are not unusual among leaders, especially among those of an intellectual capacity not matched by their followers. There are twentieth century Oxford graduates who have established regimes by force in similar fashion. It seems probable that Glyn Dwr sacrificed his own personality during the struggle to assert his authority over a force of undisciplined rebels. There could be no clemency for enemies of the Welsh, as his strength would have crumbled at the first sign of weakness.

The army marched on to Caerfyddin, where other loyalists joined Glyn Dwr. Among these were Rhys Ddu, or Rhys the Black of Aberteifi; Rhys Gethin the Fierce, hero of Pilleth, from the Vale of Conwy; Henry Don of South Wales, a man to whom Glyn Dwr had written as a friend immediately after the first tremor; and William Gwyn of Kidwelly who was a landowner in the Caerfyddin district whose intentions had been regarded as loyal to the King, until now.

Their followers swelled the numbers of the rebel army, which displayed an intimidating solidarity to those who were defending strategic, but isolated, positions in the locality. Frantic letters were sent from distraught wardens to inform King Henry that his castles were besieged, attacked and very vulnerable.

The Keeper of Newcastle Emlyn (Castell Newydd Emlyn), Jenkin ap Llywelyn, prudently chose to surrender without a fight. This opportune gift opened up the route to the North, and Welsh forces increased their attacks on Caerfyrddin town and castle, secure in the knowledge that the road was safely held in the rear should they need to withdraw quickly. On 6th July the Welsh were given the keys of Caerfyrddin by a defeated and terrified castellan, Wigmore, who saw no point in prolonging the fight against such a host.

Glyn Dwr's main force marched on towards Pembrokeshire, seizing the initiative by advancing rapidly upon an area where he knew he would encounter real opposition from the resident Flemings. On they went, camping at St Clears (San Clêr) on 9th July to reach Laugharne on 10th July.

Anticipating a swift agreement, as had happened at Castell Newydd Emlyn, Owen proposed terms of surrender to Thomas, Lord Carew, who held the castle for the King. The Welsh were anxious to return to Caerfyrddin where they had left their plunder, and they were bursting with confidence at the ease of their conquest so far. Undaunted by the opposition, unimpressed by the show of strength, Carew prepared to fight.

The Welsh had learned by this time to secure a means of retreat before attacking any English forces, a strategy which they attempted to use in this case. Owen's captains were now more experienced, and more confident, but the easy victories of the last few days had made them careless. The rebel army had grown considerably; there were more professional soldiers in the ranks than there had been at the start of the uprising at Carrog. But they underestimated their adversary.

While their leaders negotiated, exchanging terms, the Welsh followed an established procedure and on the night of 11th July sent a small group to reconnoitre the surrounding hills. The soldier Carew had anticipated such a venture, and his forces surprised the rebels in a clever ambush. Seven hundred Welsh were slain.

A soothsayer in Caerfyrddin had prophesied Glyn Dwr's downfall and hinted at his possible death "somewhere on the Gower Peninsula". Carew's victory forced Owen to change his plans, and the Welsh army moved elsewhere, their successful and jubilant progress halted either by the show of English strength or by the fear of the prophecy. The leader was not taken prisoner and dragged away "beneath a black banner" as Hopkin ap Thomas had "seen", but he did not take any risks. This retreat was providential for the people of Gower who were thus saved by the quick-thinking of their local magician, and by the magnetic lure of booty at Caerfyrddin which drew the rebels back to relative safety away from Lord Carew.

The 10th of July was to herald another change, of vital importance to the Cause, yet surrounded by uncertainty and speculation.

Hotspur was based at Chester, having completed his business in the North. Young Henry was in the Shrewsbury area after several ineffectual sorties into North Wales, hoping to march on towards Harlech as soon as he had enough funds to pay his men. King Henry was on his way to Scotland, marching to help the Percies, or so he believed. Glyn Dwr was at Laugharne, discussing terms with Carew. This was the day that Henry Percy chose to start another rebellion, assisted by his uncle the Earl of Worcester and by the trusting people of Cheshire and the Marches who still believed in the restoration of Richard II. The fact that the Northumberlands had put Henry on the throne did not seem to matter. The men of Cheshire were quite happy to push Henry off the throne, even if their leader was that same Northumberland, or rather, his son. Possibly Hotspur told the Welsh recruits that they would be helping Glyn Dwr to his rightful place, as there would soon be a Mortimer as King, and Mortimer was now part of Glyn Dwr's family. They were all linked by marriage—the Mortimers, the Percies and Glyn Dwr—and they would soon put the country back in order. This had been the agreement.

The Cheshire archers were renowned throughout England, and they had formed an important section of Richard's army. Although they had, reportedly, ripped off their white hart badges and slunk home after Richard's capture, the men of the Chester region were still feared for their military skill. Answering Hotspur's call to arms they must have been an impressive sight, with the result that many Welshmen of the Marches rushed to join Hotspur's forces. Perhaps they believed that their antagonist would be the young Prince Henry, a green youth in the eyes of seasoned campaigners, whose only fame rested on his excursions into North Wales which had not so far been particularly heroic or effective. Perhaps news had come from the south-west, where Glyn Dwr's forces were meeting resistance and achieving daily successes. In North Wales the rebels were undoubtedly in control, with all the major castles under siege, the English garrisons starving, and the Welsh waiting to pounce at the first signs of weakness.

The Northumberlands had lost faith in Henry for various reasons, in addition to his failure to ransom Mortimer. The King had demanded their captives after the Battle of Homildon Hill in Scotland, captives held for ransom by the Percies. Such ransoms were the profits of war for the lords involved in any campaign, an accepted, traditional part of their contract. Henry had also refused to pay the Percies a considerable amount of money earned from their position as Wardens of the Marches, and he had been slow to reimburse Hotspur for the expenses of protecting North Wales.

Accompanying Hotspur in his bid for power were many noblemen from the Lowlands of Scotland, men who were willing to fight the English at any and every opportunity. These valuable auxiliaries included the Earl Douglas who had been taken prisoner at Homildon Hill. This new alliance against the English King seems to indicate that Henry Percy had a special agreement with his Northern neighbours, and former enemies. The continual disruption along the border was expensive, and both sides had everything to gain if their differences could be settled by dethroning Henry. By assisting Northumberland's son, Douglas and his fellow hostages could save themselves the price of the ransom and negotiate some sort of settlement which would restore peace in the North.

The Percies, Glyn Dwr and Mortimer had already discussed a plot to overthrow the House of Lancaster, but Hotspur's sudden decision on 10th July caused a problem of communications. He also underestimated both King Henry, the veteran soldier, and his brilliant son, Prince Hal.

Hotspur began his march with the intention of capturing Prince Henry, believed to be in North Wales or travelling through the Marches towards his base at Shrewsbury. The heir to the throne would have been a valuable bargaining-piece, but the army did not find him. On 13th July the King was at Nottingham, on his way to meet the Percies on the Northern Border, after arranging for additional forces to assist the Prince who had requested troops for an attack on the Welsh at Harlech. News of the rebellion at Chester must have come as a great personal blow to the King. Tired of wars, tired of endless disputes, and always aware that the throne he held was not truly his, Henry's reign was plagued by rebels and uprisings. He must have felt that the years of unrest were some sort of divine punishment for the murder of his cousin.

Swiftly he travelled to Burton-on-Trent, and on 16th July he called up the men from the twelve counties to supplement his forces. They reached Shrewsbury on 20th July, where Prince Henry was waiting, just in time to close the gates against the approaching army led by Hotspur. Still loath to fight a former friend, Henry attempted to parley, but for Hotspur there was no reversion.

The battle was fought on Battlefield just outside Shrewsbury on 21st July, 1403. Henry Percy, the gallant, hot-headed northern warrior was killed. Many other brave men died that day as the King's forces overwhelmed the rebels, a battle described by Shakespeare in *Henry IV, Part One* as an illustration of Prince Henry's valour against the fierce onslaught led by mighty Hotspur. Battles on this scale were rare. The King had mustered the levies from a wide area, in addition to the force he had collected for his march to Scotland, and reports state that his army numbered 30,000. Hotspur was leading some 15,000, a mixed force of Welsh, Scots and the Cheshire archers.

Prince Henry was in command of the left flank, where he was obliged to fight uphill, against a hail of arrows, which must have seemed an impossible task. His chief opponents were childhood friends; Hotspur himself had been his guardian and trusted mentor. The Cock of the North had been his advisor, his father's deputy, during those important years of boyhood when Henry Percy had been responsible for the boy-prince at Chester such a short time before. Thomas Percy, Earl of Worcester, had also been the Prince's guardian, that very year.

Anger and bitterness at their treachery drove the Prince on

to merciless victory. There was fierce fighting which lasted the whole of that summer afternoon until nightfall when there was such confusion that no-one could be sure of the outcome. The Scots fought with desperate fury, welcoming the chance to slay their hated enemies, the English. Earl Douglas was captured. Prince Henry was wounded in the face by an arrow, but his courageous behaviour and refusal to leave the field encouraged his men to greater efforts. Shrewsbury (1403) was to be the dress-rehearsal for Agincourt (1415). King Henry emerged victorious at the end of a long and bloody day, his crown safely established by force of arms, with few to survive the slaughter to retain any hope of dislodging the House of Lancaster.

Those brave noblemen who died that terrible afternoon were buried in Shrewsbury churchyards. With them perished all Plantagenet hopes. The other corpses, unidentified, or unidentifiable, were placed in mass graves at the site, both loyalists and rebels together. Henry later acknowledged their sacrifice by ordering the construction of a church, where masses could be said for the souls of the slaughtered soldiers at the site where their bones had been placed. But his dead enemy, Henry Percy, was not treated with such reverence.

Hotspur's hated corpse was disinterred and publicly displayed in the marketplace at Shrewsbury, before the head was hacked off to be spiked on the North Gate at York. The King had learned a lesson. Nobody was ever going to insist that this enemy was alive as they had whispered that Richard Plantagenet still breathed. The hasty warrior's empty sockets gazed helplessly northwards, warning others that King Henry was now invincible. Buzzing flies now occupied the skull where thoughts of treason had once swarmed.

While Prince Henry was recovering from his wound, responsibility for affairs in Wales was divided between the Earl of Arundel and Glyn Dwr's longstanding antagonist, Charlton the Lord of Powys. In the deceptive calm after Shrewsbury, Henry did not forget that the hydra had other heads, and Wales was still a problem to be solved.

It is hard for anyone now to imagine the savagery and ferocity of close combat, and harder still to understand the motives that drove men to fight in pitched battles such as that at Shrewsbury when they were almost certainly outnumbered by two to one.

Why did Hotspur act so hastily? He had arrived in Chester

on 9th July and immediately proceeded to gather an army, an overt act of treason, particularly as a proclamation was issued stating that Richard II was still alive and could be seen with his troops at Chester. When Thomas Percy the Earl of Worcester joined him the combined force began its march south along the Oswestry road.

Where were his allies, Mortimer and Glyn Dwr? A pact between these leaders must have been agreed in principle during 1402-3, an agreement which determined new boundaries to be shared between the Percies, Mortimer, and Glyn Dwr as Prince of the Cymry. Their support would have meant success, as Hotspur very nearly won the day against tremendous odds.

Hotspur's own judgement must be questioned, since he must have known that his own father was too far away to assist him at that time. He knew also that Prince Henry was active in North Wales, and Glyn Dwr's tactics would have ensured that the main Welsh forces were far away in the South. News of their victories would have raced across the country, indicating the Welsh position. A guerilla leader does not face the enemy on the enemy's chosen ground, a fact which Hotspur must also have known after long acquaintance with the Welsh leader. With fatal consequences, Hotspur underestimated King Henry and the young Prince, which meant that he was forced to engage in an open fight. The King acted quickly, mustered large forces at short notice, and moved out to battle before Hotspur was ready. Great soldier that he was, the obstinate and mighty Percy could not retreat, even though he needed more time to consolidate his army. His father was on the way, or so he presumed. Mortimer and Glyn Dwr could not be too distant, perhaps within a day's march. Some accounts state that four thousand Welshmen were sent, while Glyn Dwr remained at Oswestry. Others assert that Glyn Dwr decided not to trust the Percies, or Mortimer, as they were English and would betray their Welsh ally at the first opportunity. Yet others maintain that the Welshman feared open battle, the definitive action won, or lost, in a day, preferring skirmishes and furtive attacks rather than the finality of a fight on the field in the old "chivalric" way. None of these explanations seem to fit Glyn Dwr's character, even allowing for three years in the wilderness and the erasure of some of his earlier beliefs. A defeat for King Henry at Shrewsbury would have given the

Prince of the Cymry all that he sought, and he would have been powerful enough to ensure that the Percies kept to the agreement. The English throne would have reverted to the Mortimers, to the nephew of his son-in-law; the Welsh would have achieved separation by amicable agreement and the Percies would have won a northern kingdom. It was Hotspur's poor judgement which shattered the dream. He rejected the opportunity to engage in a protracted parley which would have won valuable time.

Where was Glyn Dwr, a nation's hero, a great soldier, a man unlikely to betray his friends and allies whether English or Scot? Was he lurking behind a tree afraid to fight? And where was Mortimer? The most likely explanation seems to be that events moved too quickly, and that news travelled too slowly. King Henry knew of the revolt on 10th July and reached Shrewsbury to intercept the traitors on 20th July. Hotspur's incomplete army arrived at the same town on the twentieth after an unsuccessful attempt to intercept Prince Henry. It would have been easy for Glyn Dwr to reach Shrewsbury from Caerfyrddin within those ten days, if the news of Percy's insurrection on the tenth reached him. However, if the Welsh leader had prior knowledge that there was to be this open revolt by Hotspur and his family, with the prospect of a large force marching south to join his army, then there was no need to abandon his position. His forces had been keen to remain at Caerfyrddin to share out the booty, and they suffered an ignominious setback at Laugharne on the twelfth, a defeat which would not have been known to Hotspur at Chester. Did the men disobey their leaders and leave Glyn Dwr with insufficient troops to assist his ally? They would have been difficult to handle if their rewards were denied. Perhaps he believed that Hotspur would wait at Chester until all the allies were united under one banner. Many of the Welsh soldiers would not have been happy about fighting alongside English troops, and time was needed to accustom them to the idea.

Perhaps the messengers never came, or did not come in time, leaving Glyn Dwr with the dreadful choice of hastening to Shrewsbury with a grumbling army, or of leading them slowly knowing that Hotspur would be left to face Henry alone. Hotspur himself may have had other motives. A victory without the Welshmen would have meant more power for the Percies, helped by their friends, the Scots. There was the possibility that with young Mortimer on the throne, his nephew as well as Glyn Dwr's relative by marriage, the House of Northumberland would have been supreme regent. There are many imponderables, none of which explain Hotspur's hasty action or Glyn Dwr's inaction.

Shakespeare noted the fact that Glyn Dwr was absent, and that Mortimer had failed to arrive, in Act IV, scene iv:

> *"What with the sickness of Northumberland,*
> *Whose power was in the first proportion,*
> *And what with Glendower's absence thence,*
> *Who with them was a rated sinew too*
> *And comes not in, o'er-ruled by prophecies . . ."*

and:

> *"No, Mortimer is not there (Shrewsbury) . . ."*

The Caerfyrddin prophecy had obviously become public knowledge, and is used to suggest that Glyn Dwr rated omens higher than promises. After the battle, in Act V, scene v, Henry says:

> *"Myself, and you, son Harry will towards Wales,*
> *To fight with Glendower and the Earl of March."*

He sends his other son, John of Lancaster, to York with orders to intercept the Earl of Northumberland. After Hotspur's death, there was no opposition from his father who gave himself up to the King's mercy; thus the Earl lived to fight another day.

The Battle of Shrewsbury, although it involved Welshmen from the Marches, was more like an island in the stream of Welsh affairs, interrupting but not halting the drift. Henry's victory gave him a false feeling of security. Anyone who had been present at that dreadful slaughter must have felt that the Welsh uprising was finished except for sweeping up the ashes. So many good men had been slain that day; the most celebrated soldiers killed, executed or maimed; their traitorous followers scattered and demoralised. The cowardly Glyn Dwr had not even shown his face. At least Hotspur had died a soldier's death and many of his enemies could testify that he had fought with valour. The King could not believe that there was any further Welsh threat now that Glyn Dwr's ally was dismembered, his rotting flesh decorating the gates of five English cities, Bristol, Chester, London, Newcastle and York. Along the borders large numbers of Welshmen sought the pardons which were offered as an inducement; Henry longed for peace.

While Henry was engaged in the North of England, accepting Northumberland's apologies and patching up a reconciliation with the Percies whose help he needed along the northern Marches, the Welsh were free to continue their campaigns. Perhaps the King would have been wiser to follow Shakespeare's time-table and settle affairs in the west in the immediate aftermath of Shrewsbury.

During August Glyn Dwr's forces were active throughout Wales, and while his captains terrorised the people in the Bristol Channel area he personally travelled to the districts around Flint, to arouse enthusiasm and put new heart into those who were contemplating desertion. His forces appeared along the Shropshire border, where many feared a Welsh invasion. They were sighted near Chester, and in the Wirral, increasing in strength and ferocity. Once again letters were sent to the King from worried gentlemen who feared for their lives and lands, urging Henry to take definite action before it was too late. In Herefordshire the landowners were suffering as Welsh rebels stole and looted indiscriminately, ignoring the partial truce which had existed after Mortimer's alliance. The rich pickings were too much of a temptation.

The King was compelled to lead an army into Wales, despite his flagging energies and unwillingness to begin another campaign. He issued orders to those who held castles to take every precaution, which may seem a rather belated appeal in the circumstances. There were many privately-owned castles, however, as well as those belonging to the crown which were already in a state of readiness, provisioned and garrisoned.

During these weeks the King was undergoing severe financial difficulties. For some time he had been engaged in one uprising after another, marching round his kingdom from south to north to west and round again in an eternal triangle of hate. It may have been this shortage of money which made his advance into South Wales largely ineffective and his sojourn extremely brief. He was so desperate for funds that he even approached the Church, but a richly-clad Archbishop of

Canterbury defended the wealth of his calling by promising eternal damnation to any who tried to commandeer the tempting contents of God's houses, or His ministers' sacred possessions. Relenting a little, the Archbishop made a donation, enough to pay for the upkeep of one castle and Henry had to be satisfied.

The army marched quickly, from Hereford through Hay-on-Wye, Talgarth, Aberhonddu, Defynnog and on to Caerfyrddin with no opposition. The countryside had already suffered at the hands of the rebels, and Henry's army found little comfort along the route. Those who rushed to assure the King of their allegiance were rewarded; those who were captured as traitors were put to death, their lands confiscated and their families disgraced. Many "loyalists" were presented with the lands of their neighbours, a proven policy which ensured denouncement and betrayal. By October Henry was able to return to Hereford, leaving the Earl of Somerset in command at Caerfyrddin where the town was once again in English hands.

Almost before the last English hoof had crossed the border, the invisible rebels renewed their attack in the South. The castle at Caerfyrddin had been re-garrisoned under Somerset's command, but the men were short of supplies and John Beaufort was short of confidence. As Welsh forces attacked repeatedly, Beaufort sent desperate pleas for reinforcements and a replacement commander.

Caerdydd Castle was in such danger that urgent plans were made for a relief-force to sail from Somerset, to help the besieged garrison by crossing the Severn. By using this route the English hoped to arrive fresh and without loss of time.

Along the south coast of England, French pirates were adding to the problem by raiding towns such as Plymouth and Salcombe, although Henry had negotiated a peaceful settlement with France. The presence of hostile ships in the area hindered plans to use a sea-route, and the French began to take an active part in the Welsh struggle. On 3rd October, Henry Don, an old friend of Glyn Dwr's, was joined by French troops in an attack on Kidwelly. The un-co-ordinated force was not successful and after inflicting some damage to the town's walls, the men proceeded to terrorise the unfortunate souls who lived outside the protection of the town itself by ravaging the countryside before withdrawing.

Glyn Dwr commanded the North, where support was strong. His men continued their long sieges and sporadic assaults on the castles of the western coast, so that he virtually contained and controlled all the main English strongholds from Caerdydd up to Beaumaris in Anglesey. The numbers of this rebel army were now so large that they caused great consternation among the dejected garrisons who felt themselves totally abandoned. While Glyn Dwr led one itinerant force, his captains had individual control over numerous platoons, or groups, of rebels, so that unceasing action could be maintained in several areas simultaneously. In South Wales alone, his followers in arms were said to number up to 30,000. Lightly clad and armed, they were capable of moving from place to place at great speed, an attribute which may have made the numbers appear much greater than they actually were. It is apparent from some of their failures that while the archers and spear-men were formidable when engaged in sudden, brief on-slaughts, their weapons were not suitable for attacking the walls of great castles. After initial attacks to frighten the defending garrisons, the Welsh seem to have withdrawn before pressing home any advantage. This unsatisfactory method of fighting had been noted by Gerald of Wales in the twelfth century, when it had been equally inconclusive. In the North, the Welsh did use siege equipment, but this was only possible because they had time to settle down for a long operation, unhindered by any English reinforcements.

Some of their successes were due to cowardice on the part of their adversaries, and the castles which did succumb usually did so because of famine, or epidemic, or fear—or a combination of these three.

So, while some attacks were successful, others failed. There were many highly capable and loyal commanders among the English, particularly in South Wales and along the Marches, but they lacked supplies and men. The balance favoured the Prince of the Cymry, and he was no longer alone. His new ally, France, had begun to provide substantial aid.

After the Welsh-Gallic attack on Kidwelly, the French sailed North unhindered, to attack Caernarfon in November. The fleet patrolled Cardigan Bay and the Lleyn Peninsula, bringing essential supplies to Glyn Dwr's men who were heartened and strengthened by this show of French goodwill. Under their dashing leader, Jean d'Espagne, the French made little impression on the fortress of Caernarfon, but their presence must have caused great consternation to those within the castle. A French attack was without precedent, as the English were accustomed to fighting this particular enemy on the soil of France, not within the boundaries of Britain. The defenders had no way of knowing just how many French were invading this corner of Britain, or how far they were prepared to advance. It was a stab in the back for Henry, who was still under the misapprehension that France sought peace. Wales was optimistic as the new year dawned. Events were to prove that the optimism was justified.

CHAPTER ELEVEN

Triumphant Progress

"Hang out our banners on the outward walls;
The cry is still, 'They come'; our castle's strength
Will laugh a siege to scorn."

William Shakespeare.
Macbeth
Act V scene v.

EDWARD I's castles commanded important regions, and he had prudently populated the surrounding areas with loyal English families. For over a hundred years, Welsh and English had lived in amity, both nationalities gaining from the association, deriving benefits from the inter-change of ideas and business methods. Prosperity accompanied the merchant settlers. Thriving markets had been established in the boroughs, where increased trade brought security and new prospects to the indigenous Welsh. Although governed by English magnates, the Welsh tenants still held their lands by right of tenure as they had done before the Edwardian Conquest. The little towns of western Wales had begun to develop into sizeable communities, where goods could be bought and sold on a scale previously unknown in this untamed and rural land. Those who welcomed such economic growth found themselves opposed to the Welsh patriots, whose lawlessness was reducing the countryside to ashes. The people of Conwy had resented the intrusion of Welsh rebels and had breathed a sigh of relief when Hotspur re-established English supremacy by evicting the wild brothers William and Rhys. Welsh and English had intermarried; civil war caused only misery, dividing families, arousing hatred in hearts where there had been love and unity.

Harlech Castle was held by Richard Massey of Sale in Cheshire, but he was assisted by Vivian Collier whose family were Harlech-born. Only five of the garrison were English; the rest were Welsh. They fought side by side against the supporters of Glyn Dwr.

Caernarfon Castle was held securely for the King by William of Tranmere, who had repulsed the French attack with the help of Welsh men-at-arms. Towards the end of 1403, and during the winter months under siege, William lost three of his ablest commanders, including Ieuan ap Maredudd whose brother Robert was fighting at Glyn Dwr's side. The corpse was smuggled secretly out of the castle, to prevent any atrocities, and was buried in the churchyard at Penmorfa. Owen's terrible anger at this Welshman's traitorous support of the detested English drove him to burn Ieuan's property to the ground. Had not his own beautiful manors been utterly destroyed?

Frustrated by the impregnability of Caernarfon, the rebels turned ferociously on Criccieth Castle which was held by six men-at-arms and fifty archers. One of the rebel leaders, himself a son of Eifionydd, the area now being devastated, was Ieuan ab Einion, a nephew of the famous Hywel of the Battleaxe. Hywel had been knighted on the field at Crecy after fighting so valiantly alongside the Black Prince.

Throughout 1402 and the early months to June 1403, Harlech remained virtually unscathed. Massey commanded ten men-at-arms and thirty archers, a small force quite capable of holding the intimidating rebel army at bay. In June, Massey was relieved by a new guardian, John Hennore, but within a short time this replacement was inexplicably captured by one of Owen's followers, Robin Holland of Eglwys Fach. It would be natural to assume that no-one could enter or leave a castle under siege. But men did, occasionally, emerge either to parley with the enemy, or to depart surreptitiously under cover of darkness as Owen himself did at a later date. It was, however, virtually impossible to smuggle in reinforcements and supplies, as the steep walls, and one entrance, prevented any large-scale attempt to help those inside. While Edward's defences ensured the safety of those within, they also precluded any help.

A new guardian was appointed almost immediately, and William Hunt arrived to assume command. The small garrison was slowly starving, despite an attempt to revictual the stronghold from the seaward side. There was a small gate at the bottom of the cliff which, in those days, could be approached by water, but the Welsh loyalists of Harlech promptly dissuaded any foolhardy captain from trying to land supplies.

As the rebels of Eifionydd and Ardudwy, the lands along the coast from Criccieth to Harlech, wreaked vengeance on Welsh supporters of the crown, burning the homes of local gentry, the beleaguered garrisons remained helplessly trapped within the massive walls of both castles. With great stoicism they suffered hunger and disease. French ships now prevented any provisions, or men, reaching the inmates from the Irish Sea and Cardigan Bay. There could be no help from Henry, and no mercy from the enemy. There was no alternative but to sit, to wait, and to die.

In January 1404, Hunt was also captured by Robin Holland as he ventured outside the grim walls of Harlech to discuss terms with the rebels. This may have been a pre-arranged incident as the new Constable was not trusted by his own men. Being captured was one way of escaping the deprivations of the siege. The Welsh were well-known for treachery and a captive could always plead that a promise of safe conduct had been broken.

A messenger sent to Conwy, pleading for assistance both at Harlech and Criccieth, failed in his mission and the last flame of hope for the demoralised garrisons was quenched. During the spring Harlech surrendered, providing Glyn Dwr with a mighty Welsh base. The smaller castle at Criccieth was captured and destroyed, an example to any disloyal Welsh in the vicinity that their homes would suffer a similar fate.

On Anglesey, the garrison from Beaumaris was ambushed by French forces as the unsuspecting Maredudd ap Cynwrig went about his business collecting the King's dues. French ships landed more supplies, including wine for the jubilant rebels, and guarded the Lleyn Peninsula for Glyn Dwr. The western flank was now secure, which left the Prince of the Cymry free to survey his growing territory and to plan the future with confidence.

The London Parliament's answer to the danger was to place the sixteen-year-old Prince Henry in command of all operations in Wales. He was to be assisted in the South by Edward, Duke of York; in the North by Thomas, Earl of Arundel. Parliament omitted to vote any financial assistance, which oversight must have been infuriating for the English Prince, but encouraging for Glyn Dwr.

After Criccieth and Harlech had fallen, the castle at Llanbadarn-Fawr, Aberystwyth, surrendered. Glyn Dwr now ruled that large part of Wales bounded by Caernarfon in the North and by Aberteifi in the South, although the castle at Caernarfon was not taken. Its fortifications proved too strong even for the new siege equipment and a small garrison resisted the Welsh unflinchingly. It was not necessary to waste a large force on this exercise, so it made little difference to Owen's supremacy. The few English sympathisers within the stronghold were surrounded and harmless and could be contained without much effort. There was much support from the local inhabitants of Caernarfonshire, who sided with the rebels while they were winning. Their thoughts they kept to themselves. The prospect of a Free Wales was now a distinct possibility, so it was more expedient to help, rather than hinder, Glyn Dwr's followers who had shown that disloyalty would be rewarded with destruction.

At last the Welsh Prince was able to inaugurate a separate Welsh Parliament, and to convince many of the people that they could live their lives without England's domination. It was his idea to revert to the original Assembly, an idea developed in Wales long before English King John and the Magna Carta, a method of government which ensured representation of the people. Glyn Dwr was no despot or tyrant. During the tenth century when Hywel Dda, the Good, ruled Wales, the Assembly consisted of men from each commote. Glyn Dwr summoned four men from each commote and began preparations for his new Parliament. According to a contemporary writer, Adam of Usk, the first meeting was at Machynlleth, a central town in the area under Welsh control. Tradition maintains that Owen Glyn Dwr was formally crowned during these proceedings, and that the imposing ceremony was attended by envoys from Scotland, France and Spain. The road to freedom stretched ahead.

Whether or not Glyn Dwr was crowned at Machynlleth, certainly he adopted a new device. His seal on a letter to Charles VI of France depicts the four lions rampant of Gwynedd. Previously he had used the single lion rampant of Powys, his home territory, and had been described during an early attack on Caernarfon bearing the arms of Uther Pendragon, a golden dragon on a white field. The old Wales of the Princes had been divided into the three "kingdoms" of Gwynedd in the North-West; Powys, which covered Mid Wales and the eastern section; and Deheubarth, the South. Glyn Dwr was now in full control of Gwynedd, and his power extended into Mid Wales and the South, but unity was hard to achieve.

The letter to King Charles was written on 10th May, 1404, from Dolgellau, after the full meeting at Machynlleth. In it Glyn Dwr requested supplies and more military aid. The envoys, Owen's brother-in-law John Hanmer and his Chancellor, Gruffydd Young, delivered the request from Owen, "by the grace of God, Prince of Wales", to a friendly King who was willing to help the Welsh. The revolt offered France an opportunity to harrass the English usurper without inviting a full-scale invasion of French territory. King Richard's child-bride, Isabella, was a daughter of France. She had been returned unharmed to her father after the murder of her husband and the French had threatened hostilities. Their little Queen had been dethroned by a dishonourable action, so the vague peace treaty agreed with Richard was nullified. In 1403 a French force had landed at Plymouth and burned parts of the town. French ships patrolled the English Channel. Described as corsairs there was no official reprimand from the French court to dissuade these sailors from helping themselves to English goods, although those in authority continued lengthy peace proposals on another level. Any outright declaration of war was to be avoided, but minor irritations were encouraged.

Gifts of armour were despatched to Owen, the warrior Prince of Wales, as a sign of French goodwill, while on 14th June King Charles instructed James of Bourbon and the Bishop of Chartres to arrange more specific aid with the new Prince. Formalities were concluded in July with a firm alliance binding the two countries. The paper-work took a little longer; even in those days bureaucracy hastened slowly. As a sign of good faith, the French were immediately given details of Welsh ports and land-routes to assist their invasion forces. A large fleet set sail in August.

While these negotiations were taking place, Henry was not very active, and although many castles still remained in English hands, under siege, the Welsh were busy attacking the Border counties, strengthening their grip on areas they now controlled absolutely. Imprisoned within their strongholds of Caernarfon, Beaumaris, Conwy, Rhuddlan, Denbigh, Flint, Oswestry and Y Trallwng, Henry's garrisons could do nothing except concentrate on repelling attacks and resolve to stay alive. The King still lacked money to pay a permanent force to guard the Marches, a fortuitous situation for the rebels who were free to roam as they pleased. Outside castle or town walls, no man could travel in safety.

In June, Prince Henry had made his headquarters at Worcester after the rebels had attacked Archenfield, a district near Monmouth (Trefynwy) town. Levies from four counties were summoned to Hereford to assist, as it was feared that there would be an attack on Abergavenny.

Under the command of Richard Beauchamp, the new young Earl of Warwick, the Hereford force moved into the area to drive out the marauders. At Campstone Hill, near Abergavenny, the Welsh were forced to stand and fight. Their defeat halted any further advance into territory where they had been enjoying heady success, and Warwick was able to show that the Welsh were no match for English soldiers when fighting face to face, news which bolstered English confidence. It was reported that the leader himself had almost been captured and that the English did in fact take possession of his banner. This was a severe setback for Owen who withdrew his forces to the safer countryside around Usk and Caerleon.

Not long afterwards Glyn Dwr was able to redress the balance and retrieve some of the lost prestige by chasing the English back to the gates of Trefynwy after a skirmish at Craig y Dorth in the Trothy Valley. This engagement took place south of Trefynwy, along the route from Trelleck (Trelech) to Tintern, showing that Welsh soldiers were swarming all around the southern parts of Wales right down to the Severn and east to the English border.

During August, sixty French ships sailed gaily up and down the English Channel, and returned to France in November, without even approaching the Welsh coast. The Count of La Marche preferred posturing to campaigning and Glyn Dwr's efforts to clear the way for an invasion were wasted.

It was during this month that the people of Shropshire gratefully signed a truce with Owen's forces, and paid protection money in the hope that their lands would be spared. Even Y Trallwng, which was guarded by the mighty Castle of Pole, requested a truce so that their lives would not suffer too much disruption. The Welsh of Y Trallwng remained loyal to Henry throughout the revolt, and they had no wish to cross to the other side; nor did they wish to see their prosperity harmed by roving outlaws. Gold bought uneasy peace, but it was better than constant fear and worry that their property would be burned or their crops and animals purloined.

Glyn Dwr himself was in Caerdydd during these last weeks of summer, controlling the castle and the town, possibly anticipating the French forces which never came. Throughout Glamorgan his men brought terror to those who held out for the King. Coity Castle was in imminent danger, and hurried plans were being made by Prince Henry for its relief. Coity Castle, north of Bridgend, was isolated in the Ogmore Valley, surrounded by Welsh supporters on every side. Glamorgan resounded to the trampling feet and the cries of jubilant Welshmen, who daily expected to see French allies marching to join their army.

Owen's secure position as crowned Prince of Wales, ally of France, persuaded many more to join him. The loyalty of landowners in troubled times is fickle. While the peasants and hardened soldiers were quick to rally to their leader without hesitation, spurred on by a vision of Free Wales, many landowners were quick to adapt their patriotism depending on the current situation. It was expedient to bow the knee to whoever was winning, and the victor, for the time being, was Owen Glyn Dwr.

Churchmen were similarly inclined, self-preservation overcoming their loyalties, and there are examples of sudden allegiance, or betrayal, among men whose inconstancy was shameful.

Before the end of 1404, Prince Owen had acquired a new, and important follower in the dignified person of John Trevor, Bishop of St Asaph. The Trevors were a powerful Border family whose hearts and swords were with the Lancastrian King. John Trevor had served Henry loyally, and his cathedral at St Asaph had been burnt and ransacked by Welsh troops early on in the revolt. But now he joined Glyn Dwr, the baron who had dared to question Lord Grey's actions and prompted Trevor's sage warning that the Welsh would not be pacified. It might be considered uncharitable to suggest that the Bishop had nothing to lose, a prelate without a see, so it should be said that he became a trusted emissary and friend whose commitment to the Cause was total. Some quality in his personality won Trevor the love and admiration of Glyn Dwr's bard, Iolo

Goch, who wrote an affectionate and glowing tribute to his master's converted sympathiser. The Bishop's intelligence and knowledge of diplomacy were soon put to good use.

With the onset of winter, military activities slowed down. In the North, sieges were maintained as the rebels dug themselves in and made their quarters more comfortable in readiness for the inevitable snows and storms. In the South, small groups roamed the countryside, making sporadic attacks to remind the faint-hearted of their presence. During this lull, Prince Henry and his younger brother Prince Thomas left Hereford and marched unchallenged to Coity Castle with reinforcements and supplies. After this minor expedition, the Princes returned to their more congenial headquarters at Hereford. Supplies were also arranged for the garrisons of Kidwelly, Llanstephan and Caerfyrddin to ease their dismal winter of deprivation.

It can be assumed that Glyn Dwr also retreated to a haven of warmth and security, for some of the winter period at least, to Harlech Castle, where family and friends awaited their beloved leader. As a new sovereign, there were affairs of state to occupy his time; he could safely leave the fighting to others, for a while. From Harlech it is a short journey to Aberystwyth and the Prince could check that his two greatest material acquisitions were being adequately guarded and maintained.

In January, 1405, the treaty with France was optimistically ratified, formally signed at the castle of Llanbadarn-Fawr, Aberystwyth. The document was despatched to Charles VI and soon afterwards the French endorsed the agreement.

During February, 1405, with Glyn Dwr safely established as Prince of Wales, a new alliance was made—or an old one revived—between Owen, the Earl of Northumberland, the Lord Bardolph and Mortimer. Bardolph was one of the King's trusted councillors and the Earl of Northumberland had miraculously regained his former position by disowning the actions of his son, Hotspur. Like the first Tripartite Indenture, this plan proposed a division of territory after Henry's death which would give Mortimer the English throne, Northumberland the lands from the Midlands to the North, and Glyn Dwr the Border shires to add to his beloved Wales. The pact was concluded at Bangor on 28th February, and was probably arranged by Bishop Trevor and Bishop Byford of Bangor.

There is some confusion concerning the date of this agreement, since discussion on these lines must have taken place before Hotspur's ill-fated revolt at Chester. Shakespeare quotes the division of land in *Henry IV, Part One* before the Battle of Shrewsbury. There had been communication between Wales and the North which seems to uphold this surmise. The Bangor agreement was possibly to consolidate an alliance which had fallen into abeyance and to re-define the new "kingdoms" at a time when the Welsh were proving that Henry could be beaten. Although they had all failed to support Hotspur at the crucial time, there was obviously no animosity between Northumberland, Glyn Dwr and Mortimer.

Significantly, in February, there was an attempt to bring England's rightful heir to the safety of Mortimer lands on the marches, almost certainly with the intention of enlisting the help of Glyn Dwr. The sister of the King's trusted commander, the Duke of York, was Lady Despencer whose inherited lands were in Monmouthshire. She was guardian to the two young boys whose existence threatened Henry's sovereignty, not by rebellion or armed revolt, but by their innocent, dangerous blood-line. The boy Earl of March was the undeniable heir to the throne; his younger brother was next in line of succession. Their lives had not been threatened, but they were kept under supervision, closely guarded. They had spent Christmas at Windsor and it was not difficult to arrange their escape while the King and his court were elsewhere.

Lady Despencer* and the two boys managed to reach Gloucestershire. They had only to cross the Severn to find safety and seek help from their late father's brother, Uncle Edmund Mortimer, brother of Lady Percy and son-in-law of Glyn Dwr. Sadly they were re-captured. The ignoble lady denounced her own brother who was sent to the Tower. The opportunity to thrust Richard's lawful heir into prominence as a rallying-point was forever lost. Perhaps Mortimer would have used the boys as tools for his own ambition and they were safer with Henry. The Earl of March appears to have been singularly unambitious; he remained in virtual obscurity, treated humanely but with suspicion, a permanent reminder to the King that his position was illegal. When Prince Henry became King, he was able to use the Earl in his campaigns against France, trusting him as a commander in his army.

*Constance, Lady Despencer lived with the Earl of Kent after her husband, the Earl of Gloucester, was beheaded at Bristol in 1400.

The failure to release the brothers from the King's custody, and Lady Despencer's subsequent disgrace, had no effect on the affairs of the Welsh, Mortimer and the Scots. They made their compact and prepared to renew hostilities with the coming of fine weather in the spring. The road to independence stretched ahead.

CHAPTER TWELVE

Some Glory; Some Grief

"*Upon my life, my lord,*
The powers that you already have sent forth
Shall bring this prize in very easily.
To comfort you the more, I have receiv'd
A certain instance that Glendower is dead."

William Shakespeare.
Henry IV, Part Two.
Act III scene i.

DURING March, 1405, a Welsh attack near the River Monnow was thwarted by Herefordshire men. A large rebel force of eight thousand led by Rhys Gethin had rampaged through Glamorgan, prudently avoiding the stronghold of Abergavenny, to descend ferociously on the slumbering town of Grosmont. After the enforced idleness of winter, the Welsh indulged themselves enthusiastically in an orgy of looting and indiscriminate burning, terrorising the peaceful populace of the prosperous community. Their jubilation was short-lived.

English troops were moved quickly from Hereford to assist Prince Henry of Monmouth, now eighteen years old and determined to prove the superiority of the House of Lancaster. Accompanied by experienced knights such as Gilbert Talbot of Goodrich, William Newport and John Grendor, the Prince led his disciplined army from Grosmont Castle and forced the Welsh to stand and fight. At the end of the day, hundreds of men from Gwent and Glamorgan lay dead. The majority had been forced to flee, pursued by the victorious Prince, unable to withstand the onslaught of a resolute, confident English army. This defeat was a devastating blow to the patriots, and the rash Rhys Gethin, hero of Pilleth, must shoulder the blame. This time the Welsh archers in Prince Henry's forces did not switch their allegiance. Those who stayed to fight were hacked down. Prince Henry's report to his father barely conceals his gleeful satisfaction, and the glad tidings were immediately proclaimed to the people of London, to reassure them that they were safe from the renegades over the border, and to demonstrate that the heir to the throne of England was worthy of his position.

Seeking to redress the balance, Owen attempted to re-group his scattered forces and to re-possess the lost territory. The English had relentlessly pushed to the Castle of Usk, which was now held by Lord Grey of Codnor assisted by John Grendor, who had apparently rid the whole area of Welsh supporters. Glyn Dwr's son, Gruffydd, led an abortive attack on the castle. The rebels were repulsed and withdrew, to be chased by the defenders to a rise outside the town called Mynnydd Pwll Melyn, The Hill of the Yellow Pool, where there was a disastrous confrontation. In the confusion of the retreat, many Welsh were killed, as English soldiers hunted them mercilessly through the forest of Monkswood, near Usk, forcing the rebels to scatter or surrender.

Gruffydd was captured, but he was more fortunate than many of his compatriots. As an important hostage his life was spared, but some three hundred Welsh were summarily executed. If this number is added to the reputed fifteen hundred slain on the battlefield, this was an unmitigated tragedy for Welsh hopes and Welsh families. Among the corpses the English soldiers were overjoyed to discover one resembling the hated Owen himself, but elusive Glyn Dwr was not yet dead. A contemporary account describes how the body was later identified as the chieftain's brother Tudor, which was a sad blow for the family but a reprieve for the Cause. There was a great physical resemblance between the brothers, Tudor, or Tudur in Welsh, had not been seriously involved in the earlier campaigns and he had been pardoned by Henry after the initial uprising in 1400. It seems probable that he had rejoined Glyn Dwr soon after this earlier defection, paying the ultimate price for fraternal loyalty at the Yellow Pool of Usk. Gruffydd was removed to the Tower of London, where he remained a prisoner for the next six years, until he died of disease in that place where so many have passed their last hours on earth.

These serious setbacks in South Wales caused many in Gwent and Glamorgan to renounce Glyn Dwr, especially as Henry offered clemency and generous pardons. The King was still a clever politician; restored lands and prosperity were far more beneficial to the crown than a countryside ravaged by

(xxv) The massive Gatehouse of Denbigh Castle.

(xxvi) Abergavenny Castle ruins.

(xxvii) The Red Castle of Pole, Y Trallwng (Welshpool).

(xxviii) Glyn Dwr's Cave near Tonfanau, Tywyn.

(xxix) The slopes of Cader Idris.

(xxx) Corwen Churchyard, another possible resting place for Glyn Dwr.

(xxxi) The wilds of Plynlimon.

(xxxii) Valle Crucis Abbey near Llangollen.

(xxxiii) Tal y Llyn Pass from the road between Dolgellau and Machynlleth.

(xxxiv) Llyn Dinas, near Castell Dinas Emrys, Beddgelert.

(xxxv) The slopes of Mynydd y Gaer at Corwen where Owain Gwynedd massed his army before marching against Henry II and where Glyn Dwr reputedly gathered his forces against Henry IV.

(xxxvi) The Vaughan family arms incorporating the Three Englishmen's Heads of Ednyfed Fychan's shield and the four lions rampant of Gwynedd.
By courtesy of Canon Elias Hughes, Llanelltyd Church

IN COELO QUIES.

(xxxvii) Plas Penmynydd, original home of Owen Tudor.

(xxxviii) Penmynydd Church, Anglesey which contains the effigy of Gronw ap Tudur.

war. It was more diplomatic to encourage repentant turncoats who would soon owe allegiance to their generous monarch, rather than breed more resentment by crushing misguided local landowners.

Yet almost the whole of North and Mid Wales was still held for Glyn Dwr, excepting those besieged castles which dotted the countryside like oases of English strength. The loyalty of the common man did not waver so easily as the loyalty of their superiors.

May was a difficult month for Owen, and Welsh confidence was tested further by the loss of Anglesey. A force led by Stephen Scrope sailed from Ireland to sneak up on the complacent rebels who had been holding the area around Beaumaris with little or no opposition. The Welsh were forced to seek refuge in Snowdonia across the Menai Straits, leaving the island to the English. Glyn Dwr's kingdom was beginning to crumble at the edges.

An unexpected reprieve allowed Wales some breathing-space. On 28th May, King Henry was obliged to postpone his planned invasion of the Principality when more urgent problems arose in the North of England. The King had been gathering levies at Hereford and Worcester, preparing for a final show of strength as warm spring weather made a large-scale incursion possible. The Earl of Northumberland, probably anticipating Henry's commitment to the Welsh business, chose that moment to join a new rebellion. Forgiven by the King, pardoned and restored to his estates after Hotspur's treachery at Shrewsbury, Northumberland the royal ally proved more untrustworthy than any of the King's overt enemies.

The leader of this new uprising was the Archbishop of York, Richard Scrope. Another confederate was Earl Bardolph, formerly one of Henry's unsuspected adherents. The Archbishop's forces numbered twenty thousand conditioned, experienced fighters, and the King saw danger. Two important Welsh churchmen were also involved, their presence indicating Glyn Dwr's participation, from a distance, in this fresh turmoil. Bishop Byford of Bangor and Bishop Trevor of St Asaph were in the North to demonstrate Welsh co-operation in the concerted attack on the House of Lancaster. War may seem a strange pastime for eminent churchmen, but the guardians of men's spiritual welfare often became embroiled in men's physical troubles, and, indeed, often encouraged warfare by implying that God approved. Churchmen were often expert schemers, their fingers were constantly sticky from delving into the political pie. They were usually men from rich and powerful families, accustomed to intrigue and the mantle of authority. This seemingly incompatible mixture of prayer and plotting, piety and politics, is apparent today in those countries which seethe and simmer in the turbulence of the twentieth century.

Without hesitation, King Henry's army hurtled to meet this threat from the North. This battle was straightforward, unlike those inconclusive skirmishes in Wales. Scrope and Northumberland were defeated at Shipton Moor in Yorkshire, with the result that Bardolph and the Earl had to turn to run for the Scottish border leaving the Archbishop in Henry's custody. The Welsh bishops departed hastily.

Scrope was executed and dismembered, in 1405. Many others were despatched with equal ferocity as an effective and salutary warning to other would-be traitors. Henry had lost patience. The King stayed in the North of England to reinforce his position there before more bad news was brought to him at Pontefract towards the end of July.

Another meeting of the Welsh Parliament was held at Harlech on 1st August, when men were once again summoned from each commote to hold a formal discussion of their country's affairs. The proceedings included the matter of the French alliance and a possible truce with England which would restore peace. A more stable situation would have enabled the Welsh to carry out their avowed intentions, to establish a Wales that was separate, self-governed and independent. The English had allowed Wales reasonable terms once before, in 1267, with the Treaty of Shrewsbury. There was every hope that this Henry would accept, and acknowledge Owen's country as a useful neighbour. There were many similarities between these parallel situations.

In 1267, Henry III was growing old and weary of the incessant troubles caused by the Welsh. He had left affairs in the hands of his son, Edward. The Welsh Prince Llywelyn had won large tracts of Welsh soil, at the expense of Marcher Lords, which were granted to him legally with the Treaty of Shrewsbury. He was then recognised as the Prince of Wales. After Henry III's death, Edward became the mighty Edward I whose castles still dominate North Wales. Henry IV was also growing older, and weary of the Welsh problem. He was suffering from a debilitating illness which prevented any decisive action to settle the irritating nuisance in the West. He had an aversion to campaigns in Wales, leaving affairs in that sodden country to his son, Prince Henry. This son was to become as famous for his military prowess as that first scourge of Wales, Edward I. Both monarchs learned their skills in the wilds of Snowdonia.

The defection of supporters in South Wales and the loss of Anglesey had not swayed the resolution, or sapped the confidence of those in the North, where both major strongholds of Harlech and Aberystwyth were held securely by the Welsh. There is evidence, however, that Glyn Dwr's Parliament was infiltrated by Welsh traitors, two gentlemen from Flint, who were to report the secret proceedings to Sir John Stanley in Cheshire.

The French fleet sailed again, and this time landed at Milffwrd after a rough Channel crossing which no doubt persuaded the French commander that Welsh soil was preferable to the mountainous seas of "La Manche." They brought a mixed force of crossbowmen and infantry to meet Glyn Dwr's muster of ten thousand patriots. News of this invasion was brought to Henry with all speed, and on 7th August he ordered a muster of English levies from eighteen shires before leaving Pontefract Castle for Leicester to organise his defences. His illness did not hinder the King when England's very security was threatened, but an army could not be gathered overnight.

Together the Welsh and French troops attacked the town of Haverfordwest (Hwiffordd), but were unable to make any impression on the castle there. At Tenby (Dinbych y Pysgod), where there was a predominantly English-speaking population, the allies began a siege of the castle, but when thirty English ships appeared in the harbour it is reported that the Welsh fled, closely followed by the French. Lord Berkeley, in command of the English fleet, destroyed some of the French ships as they lay at anchor.

To regain some of their lost prestige after this cowardly exhibition, the rebels managed to capture Caerfyrddin town and castle. Once again the luckless town changed hands. Aberteifi and much of the surrounding district also succumbed before local and foreign forces reunited, and the mixed army marched eastwards towards Hereford, achieving some small successes on the way before they arrived at Woodbury Hill near Worcester.

Once again the King moved with commendable speed, arriving at Worcester on 22nd August at the head of a huge English army. More levies arrived daily, and the Welsh-French soldiers found themselves awaiting a battle on the open ground they had sought to avoid. Welsh spearmen and archers were an unlikely combination with French crossbowmen. The guerillas found themselves linked with French infantry who knew only one way to fight a battle; it was a situation not to their liking. They had few supplies, with no hope of additional food and fodder for their animals as they were in a hostile and already depleted area. They were not in a good position to attack, or defend. By 29th August there had been a few skirmishes between foraging-parties and opposing reconnoitre groups, and King Henry prepared to advance. It would have been a decisive battle. The English knights encased in steel armour, their banners waving jauntily, anticipated a victory with honour, another Crecy fought on English fields. They would destroy Welsh and French in one glorious day.

Glyn Dwr retreated. This was not the type of warfare he wanted. His army of wild Welshmen were accustomed to swift raids and crafty attacks launched from their mountain-bases. They had not fared so well during their more recent exchanges against disciplined English forces in the open. The French were able fighters, flamboyantly courageous, acknowledged masters of their weapons, the crossbows. They were probably anxious to defeat the English in the name of France. But they were mercenaries and Glyn Dwr had learned many lessons during his hard career, chief of which must have been to trust none but himself and his own men, and even that trust was qualified. He had gained other victories through treachery, and knew well that men could switch their allegiance, or desert, at the first sign of defeat. The French had their own reasons for hating the English; the Welsh were not renowned for their steadfastness. The Welsh leader was intelligent enough to realise that he was leading an army of diverse loyalties, and temperaments. Henry's forces were seasoned veterans, well-paid and well-fed. They were Englishmen who were only too happy to fight French and Welsh invaders. There were also many Welsh fighters on Henry's side, deadly archers led by great knights who had fought continually over a period of years, gaining valuable experience as they defended king and country. There can be no doubt that they were formidable.

This was the last time that Glyn Dwr would have the opportunity to come face to face with his enemy. Leading a hungry force of mixed nationalities, mixed loyalties, and placed in the situation where they must hold an unsuitable position without supplies or reinforcements there was only one course open to him. Glyn Dwr and his army melted away into the sheltering woods and mountains of Wales, leaving Henry to claim a bloodless victory.

The English had to be content with a minor punitive expedition which was hampered by bad weather. The royal forces pushed forwards to relieve Coity Castle which had been enduring a long and miserable siege. During this storm-drenched campaign the English were constantly beaten by the elements, and ambushed by rebels from the Rhondda Valley who acted on their own initiative. They were more like Robin Hood's outlaws than seriously-minded patriots.

Frustrated, the King turned back towards Hereford. His bad luck continued. During floods which followed severe storms, the royal baggage-train was lost as Welsh bandits took advantage of the downpour to seize the valuables and kill some of the King's troops. Swollen rivers had compelled the men to halt, and the Welsh slew them as they sought hopelessly for safe crossing-places. It was a dejected and demoralised monarch who returned to England at the beginning of October after thankfully leaving affairs in Wales to the Earl of Arundel and Lord Grey of Codnor. Henry had seen enough of the Glamorgan countryside and endured enough Welsh weather to last him the rest of his life. He never again set foot in Wales.

That autumn, many of the French returned to their home land, unwilling to face a winter in the desolate, alien countryside of Wales. Their own leaders, like the English nobles, were responsible for pay and equipment, and it was expensive to keep a force of soldiers for any length of time. Some French lords had to sell property or lands in order to pay their men, a sacrifice which would not have encouraged them to stay longer in support of a foreign Prince. Some of the crossbowmen and lightly-armed troops stayed with Glyn Dwr until the following spring, doubtless grumbling at the harsh conditions of a

Welsh winter in mud and snow. In 1406, as soon as conditions for travel had improved, they too left for France. It is apparent that reports of the Welsh retreat at Worcester had persuaded the French King that the way to the English throne did not lie through Wales. Political affairs in France were already simmering, a factor which may also have caused the abrupt withdrawal of some of the French nobles. Charles VI was by now virtually insane, and his instability was to cause an outbreak of war between his brother, Louis of Orleans, and his cousin, John of Burgundy. There was to be further luke-warm aid from across the Channel, but the main ally had been lost. Before long Charles would have enough problems within his own country, and the fate of Wales would be unimportant.

Early in this year, Northumberland and Bardolph fled to Wales, seeking a safe hide-out after the flight into Scotland, and willing to continue their fight against Henry by leading Welsh forces under Glyn Dwr's command. There had been rumours that the King was prepared to exchange his Shrewsbury captive, Earl Douglas, for the hated Northumberland. Scotland was no longer safe for fugitive traitors, as pure chance had given Henry another persuasive bargaining-piece. King Robert's son, James, had been captured as he travelled to France. When Robert III died on 4th April, 1406, Henry was left holding the new King of Scotland a prisoner. Such a hostage ensured complete surrender and Scotland was forced to co-operate, leaving Wales stranded, with no major allies, becoming more and more isolated. Henry could now concentrate on the troubles in the West, secure in the knowledge that there would be no outbreak in the North while King James was in his care.

Some authorities prefer to allocate the Tripartite Indenture to this period, the early months of 1406, as Northumberland, Mortimer and Glyn Dwr were certainly at the same place to plan their campaign. However, as the document describes very fully the division of mainland Britain, after King Henry's removal, it seems more probable that the plan was made earlier when Northumberland had a great deal more to offer. His flight from Scotland had left him with no real force to back his claim to the "kingdom" of Northern England, a claim that optimistically embraced all major counties from Norfolk and Warwick to Northumberland and Westmorland.

Perhaps the three men now resurrected their original plan to divide England and Wales into three feudal states. Owen certainly remained buoyant, although his plans for an independent Cambria were still dependent on French help. In March he received a letter from Charles VI indicating that Wales could rely on military help if the Welsh would recognise the Avignon Pope, Benedict XIII, as the true Pope. Such recognition, hinted Charles, would almost certainly mean a grant of independence to the Church in Wales. Mad Charles had his moments of lucidity.

Catholic Europe was divided by what is known as the Great Schism, which lasted from 1378 to 1417. There was a Pope at Rome, and a Pope at Avignon. Both the Italians and the French wanted the Papacy, not for its religious prestige but for the money and influence which accompanied the Vicar of Christ. There were bitter feuds, and many men lost their lives in the conflict between rival factions to decide whether France or Italy should house God's representative.

Glyn Dwr, like his fellow Welshmen, had been a follower of the Pope at Rome, Boniface IX, from whom he had sought permission in 1397 for plenary remission in the hour of his death. In 1403 the Welsh Prince had again contacted Rome, and altered his request; Boniface had substituted the words "at any time" to cover the new possibility that Owen might be in need of confession at any hour in the course of his many battles. Pope Boniface died in the following year and was succeeded for a short time by Innocent VII. In 1406, the Italian Pope was Gregory XII.

However, new situations demand new allegiances, and the French Pope at Avignon, Benedict XIII, was accepted by a Welsh Parliament which met at Machynlleth at the end of March. The Avignon Pope was known to obey his King's commands so the decision was eminently sensible. The Machynlleth reply to King Charles contained many proposals which were essential for Welsh Independence, and even contained a clause which branded Henry IV as a heretic for his allegiance to the Roman Pope. The Welsh suggested that he should be tortured "in the usual manner".

The nobles and prelates who gathered at the Machynlleth Parliament had obviously given much thought to Wales' future policies. They sought Benedict's approval on several issues, in the knowledge that the Pope would follow the directions of his master, Charles VI, who had already indicated his personal co-operation.

They requested absolution for their former, misguided vows to the Pope in Rome. They sought the restoration of St David's to its original dignity, with control over the lesser churches of St Asaph, Bangor and Llandaff and those of the Marches and bordering counties such as Hereford and Worcester. Many concessions were requested on the subject of financial control within the Church, a vital issue, with Welsh-speaking Welshmen appointed to their rightful positions within dioceses. Absentee English bishops had collected the rents and revenues from Welsh sees, and many had not even visited their Welsh abbeys, preferring to remain comfortably in England awaiting the money which was due to them. It was a corrupt system, which thrived in England as well as in Wales, and churchmen grew fat on the proceeds without having to stir from their opulent homes.

While these ecclesiastical matters were extremely important to many of Owen's supporters, some of whom, like Bishop Byford of Bangor, would gain considerably by formal ratification of his shaky appointment, the proposal to create Welsh universities assumes greater significance. The universities of Oxford and Cambridge were, by this time, inaccessible. Welsh students were naturally unwelcome at any English institutions, and there was no future for them outside Wales. Laws discriminating against the Welsh had been in operation since the early years of the revolt.

The importance of education in Glyn Dwr's plans reveals a sparkling facet of this extraordinary leader's character. While historians have often dismissed the Welsh uprising as the Cambrian equivalent to the Peasants' Revolt, this proposal to establish universities must indicate that Owen was seeking more for his countrymen than better wages. His own upbringing must have conditioned his thinking. He hoped to establish two seats of learning, one in the North and one in the South.It was an admirable dream. Universities breed ideas, and the young men of Wales would have been able to dicuss new, revolutionary doctrines with impunity. Glyn Dwr had seen the effects of John Wycliffe's preaching from his base at Oxford, a heretical reformer who attacked the established church and sent itinerant Lollard preachers into the countryside to stir up discontent. Glyn Dwr did not condone Lollardy, but he had seen how one educated man could affect thousands. With Welsh universities, Welsh students could preach their ideas without hindrance, and the people of Wales would learn independence from their own sons.

The letter was sent to France on 31st March, and expectations were high. On St. George's Day, 23rd April, 1406, the English won a major victory and a thousand Welshmen were killed. One of Owen's sons perished, but the site of this defeat is not known.

In June, Northumberland and Bardolph were defeated by the military power of Edward Charlton, Lord of Powys, who had been appointed by the King to maintain peace in North Wales. Henry was growing weary, plagued by illness, exhausted by the interminable campaigns he had been forced to lead from one end of the country to the other. His affliction would have made travelling a torture, and his formerly imposing countenance was reportedly raddled by the incurable disease. The fine figure of Henry Bolingbroke was now distorted by what many described as God's punishment for his treatment of the Archbishop of York. Whether it was leprosy or venereal disease, the illness often rendered him incapable of governing, and it was rumoured that his days were numbered. His Parliament still required him to deal with affairs of state, when he was sufficiently recovered, as the affairs of Government must go on whatever other events were disrupting the country.

At the age of nineteen, Prince Henry was a veteran soldier. Although he had no major victory to his name, he was experienced and admired. He was given full authority and immediately put to use the earlier, successful tactics of his mentor, Hotspur. He offered pardons to those who would desert the army of the other Prince of Wales, his traitorous contender, Owen Glyn Dwr. It was an irresistible offer. Once again the people proved to be treacherous when there was a chance to save their skins and their lands. Without help from Scotland or France, many believed that the Cause must be doomed to failure, and Prince Henry offered an easy escape. The Gower area reverted to the English, followed quickly by Ceredigon, the district of Cardiganshire which had suffered at the hands of both English and Welsh and been invaded by the French. Enough was enough. By the end of the year Anglesey was totally under English control and the inhabitants queued to swear allegiance to Henry, vowing that the Welsh rebels had nothing to do with them. The island had been invaded during 1405 by English forces under the leadership of Stephen Scrope, son of that same Baron Scrope named in the Chester trial. Supporters of the Welsh Prince had been driven back into Snowdonia, leaving the Island of Mon, as it is known in Welsh, the granary of Wales, in the hands of the enemy. The inhabitants of Anglesey, no longer obliged to pretend allegiance to absent rebels, must have felt that their island could never be re-taken by Glyn Dwr, and the pardon left them free to continue their agricultural lives in peace.

There were heavy fines to pay, demanded by Prince Henry as punishment, but the instinct for self-preservation among Welsh landowners was stronger than their loyalty to Glyn Dwr. They preferred to pay with gold and not with their lives. By submitting to the English Prince, buying clemency, Glyn Dwr's compatriots deserted at an alarming rate and they were a major cause of the decline which inevitably followed.

Hopes of further aid from Charles VI began to fade like the insubstantial Welsh mists before the rising sun. The carefully-prepared missive from Pennal, Machynlleth, despatched in the spring, was well-received by the unstable French King, but his reply was a rather petulant rebuke. If the Welsh had only shown a little more appreciation to his French soldiers then he would not hesitate to send more aid. He really was very willing to assist his friends; but assistance did not materialise.

Towards the end of the year, Northumberland and Bardolph travelled to France, still seeking help for their lost cause, hoping that Scotland could be revitalised and that Henry could still be beaten. Such a scheme would have helped Glyn Dwr, as a French invasion in the North would have distracted the King and led to Prince Henry's withdrawal. However, events in Wales were changing Owen's fortunes. Too many of his supporters were prepared to desert and Prince Henry was not the tired old man that his father had become. Here was the future glorious soldier of England's conquests abroad, intent on the destruction of a minor Welsh baron in command of a ragged army. The English sun was rising inexorably in the East, while in the West, the Welsh dream was slipping away.

CHAPTER THIRTEEN

Castles and Kings

"From enemies heaven keep your majesty;
And, when they stand against you, may they fall
As those that I am come to tell you of!"

William Shakespeare.
Henry IV, Part Two
Act IV scene iv.

THE Welsh fought tenaciously to hold on to those diminished areas where loyalties had always been strongest. Small groups were active in many parts of South Wales, even where the local inhabitants had recently reverted to the King. They were still a danger and English strongholds were re-provisioned and provided with more equipment to ward off possible attacks. Security was not relaxed; the threat remained. Owen himself was not in evidence. Throughout the winter of 1406 and the early months of 1407, he was rumoured to be in several unlikely places, yet tradition cannot be completely ignored. The stories that describe his aimless wanderings, seen here in an abbey, there in a castle, may hold some truth. A cave at the mouth of the Dysynni River near Tywyn is reputed to have been his lair during this period. Another story places him at Valle Crucis Abbey near Llangollen, while another legend describes Glyn Dwr at Coity Castle as the guest of Lord Berkrolles, albeit unrecognised until his departure.

It does seem likely that Owen travelled in disguise, no longer flaunting the proud banner of Gwynedd. The defection of so many of his own countrymen would have endangered his valuable person. The King's reward to any man who presented him with a captive Glyn Dwr would have been worth the risk, and the contempt of the dwindling band of patriots. Owen probably needed to make a personal assessment of his strength throughout the country, and no doubt he hoped to instill renewed fervour by visiting supporters on an unheralded tour.

He certainly had no need to scurry about North Wales as a fugitive, nor did he need to risk his person in South Wales by dining incognito within the walls of Coity Castle. He, more than anyone, must have realised how valuable his own person was to the Cause.

Whatever happened elsewhere, both castles of Harlech and Aberystwyth were defended against determined English attacks. The summer of 1407 saw intense activity at Aberystwyth, where the fortress was held by Rhys Ddu, the Black, of Aberteifi. He had proved to be a ferocious commander during the years of revolt. English forces led by Prince Henry himself surrounded the castle walls. Mighty siege-machines were brought to break the resistance of Rhys' small garrison. So many noble knights accompanied the Prince that there was continual rivalry within his camp, dissension which led to the departure of some of his troops who had grown disillusioned with the hard conditions and poor rewards. They had endured untold misery in the mud, pelted by rainstorms, and they were poorly fed. Growing weary of the arguments, and seeing his forces disappearing at a steady rate, Prince Henry offered Rhys a pardon if he would surrender.

Among Prince Henry's commanders were proven soldiers such as Lord Carew, who had defeated the Welsh at Laugharne; John Grendor, who had been instrumental in the slaughter at Grosmont and at Usk; John Talbot, the Earl of Warwick and the Duke of York were present, all seeking glory and the death of the rebel leaders. Rhys, looking down from the walls of old Llanbadarn-Fawr castle, must have seen a formidable array of knights and weapons. Some of the great new cannons which had never been seen before in Wales were lined up to bombard the crumbling defences. These guns were still in their infancy, and were liable to do as much damage to the operators as to the enemy, but they were wickedly effective alongside the more traditional trebuchets. Understandably, Welsh resolution must have faltered.

On 12th September, an agreement was made to relinquish the castle after six weeks if Glyn Dwr's men could not dislodge the English troops who were surrounding the stronghold. There was great ceremony, accompanied by a solemn mass conducted by the Chancellor of Oxford University, Richard Courtenay. It was a wholly medieval, chivalric arrangement organised by the epitome of English military courtesy. Honour could be salvaged from the deadlock and everyone could go home before the winter set in.

When Glyn Dwr heard the terms of the proposed agreement, he went to Aberystwyth himself, threatening instant death to any traitors and cowards, including Rhys Ddu. He remained at the castle to put new heart into the besieged Welshmen. This drastic threat, and his own presence, forced Prince Henry to retreat rather than face a winter pacing up and down outside the impregnable walls.

Temporarily defeated he returned to England, leaving behind enough disgruntled men to maintain the siege in his absence. His journey to the border was not without mishap, as Wales' greatest natural asset, rain, pelted his retinue incessantly. Like his father, Prince Henry had reason to curse Wales and everyone in the sodden, hostile country. Some of his baggage was stolen before he reached England as his men struggled through the muddy passes to safety. While the siege prevented supplies and reinforcements from reaching the men inside, there were opportunities for an individual to escape and travel under cover of darkness across that rugged terrain which lies between the Dorey Valley in Mid Wales and the Mawddach estuary. Glyn Dwr probably returned to Harlech after he had re-established his authority, and revitalised the hopes of the trapped men.

In November, 1407, England and France signed a truce, leaving Wales to its fate. Political affairs in France had changed considerably with the murder of Louis of Orleans, the King's brother. The country was divided into opposing factions, and it became expedient to form new alliances. There would be no more help from France, no more ships to bring supplies, no French soldiers to swell the Welsh army. Northumberland and Bardolph had returned to Scotland, having realised the futility of seeking French aid after the death of their supporter, Louis, yet hopeful that they could arouse hostilities in the North even without outside assistance.

The winter of 1407-8 was the most severe ever recorded in the British Isles. Blizzards swept the mountains as Northumberland attempted to stir up a revolt along the Scottish border and in the North of England. His tenacity cannot be disputed, but that uprising was his last attempt. While deep snow lay across Britain, on 19th February, both the old Earl and Bardolph were killed at the Battle of Bramham Moor near

Tadcaster, and Glyn Dwr lost his last allies. A colder wind was blowing across Wales.

One of the prisoners taken at Bramham Moor was Bishop Byford of Bangor. He preserved his skin by wearing his robes, not armour, and thus his life was spared. Henry had suffered enough from the crime of killing churchmen, or so he believed. Byford was only one of the claimants to the bishopric of Bangor. Church affairs generally were in a state of some confusion in Wales after Glyn Dwr's French alliance which had switched allegiance from Rome to Avignon.

One of the Bangor bishops was Richard Young, a supporter of Henry IV, but like many medieval churchmen he was an absentee landlord. Byford, an ambitious parson who had ingratiated himself at the influential court of Boniface IX in Rome, applied for the vacancy in 1404, which request was granted, and he came to Wales from Rome as a supporter of the new Prince of Wales. To aggravate the English and to obtain important concessions, Glyn Dwr was persuaded to abandon Rome in order to establish his Welsh Church with powers to collect taxes and rents. The new treaty ratified existing appointments wherever these were acceptable, and Byford's dubious claim to the see of Bangor was not endangered.

It was from within the Welsh group that a rival emerged, in the person of Gruffydd Young, Archdeacon of Merioneth. Gruffydd was exceptionally clever; he was a Bachelor of Laws, whose talents were to place him at Glyn Dwr's side as Chancellor and chief advisor. He had joined Owen's campaign some time after 1401, but his early commitment to Henry was soon forgotten as he used his knowledge to promote the Welsh Cause. In 1407, Pope Benedict named Gruffydd Young as the Bishop of Bangor, and Byford appears to have trodden a separate path to the North of England. Ambition and double-dealing was not confined to politicians. Byford was imprisoned, and forfeited his remaining jewels and possessions, while yet another man was appointed to the busy bishopric of Bangor.

The year 1408 was disastrous for Glyn Dwr. Although groups of his supporters continued to cause concern among the Marcher Lords of Glamorgan, the "traitors" in North Wales had largely succumbed to the English who were offering rewards and pardons to any who would betray the Cause.

Arriving with the months of more temperate weather came

the twenty-one year old Prince Henry, Royal Deputy in Wales, to renew his attack on Aberystwyth, after his ragged withdrawal the previous year. He had to prove to Parliament, far away in London, that he, the heir to the throne, was a capable commander. After several frustrating months the siege was broken, enabling Henry to capture the castle in September. The leaders of the resistance escaped but the fortress was lost. It seems likely that the rebels were beginning to feel totally isolated and abandoned within the walls of Llanbadarn-Fawr. Aware that no relief would be forthcoming, and that Glyn Dwr was rapidly losing support, the fact that the leaders managed to disappear unscathed suggests a compromise. There are reports that the garrison was allowed to leave the castle unpunished, which seems an unusually generous gesture on Prince Henry's part after the protracted and expensive operations of the siege. As autumn approached, the end of the siege was beneficial to both sides. Prince Henry won his tedious battle, and Rhys Ddu lived to fight another day. Only one obstacle remained.

Harlech had been under constant attack from the combined forces of Gilbert and John Talbot fighting for King Henry. Not all the men of Ardudwy were English sympathisers however, and one group successfully intercepted a vessel carrying supplies for the Talbots, some of which may have found their way into the castle. Apart from this incident which may or may not have brought some relief to the inhabitants of that cold, grey stronghold, deprivation was total. There was no chance of escape.

The great walls were continually bombarded. Archers kept up a constant volley of arrows which demoralised those within. The effort required for interminable vigilance was enormous, as the prowlers on the outside were ready for any crack in the defences. There were so few within to maintain the security of the castle, as Edward I had intended, while the Talbots' large force of confident soldiers had only to wait, taunting their "captives" with the scents of roasting meat. Glyn Dwr's desperate followers must have stared hopelessly, in vain, across the sea which stretches to the western horizon and Lleyn, watching for any boat that might be bringing supplies. But there were no French ships now in Cardigan Bay. Once again, King Henry's loyal subjects from Bristol sailed the Irish Sea, carrying provisions for the English, not for the Welsh.

John Talbot, Lord Furnival, proved a formidable captain, a man who was later to prove himself in the wars against France as an antagonist facing Joan of Arc. His successes during the reign of Henry V gained him many honours, and he became Earl of Shrewsbury. His men maintained the bombardment of Harlech, using cannons to weaken the outer walls. Their blockade was unbroken throughout the autumn, as the only way to approach the castle, with the entire district occupied by English soldiers, was by sea; the Welsh had no ships. Aberystwyth had fallen, and the Talbots knew that it was only a matter of time. Within the sheltering walls were Glyn Dwr's own family, bravely defended by ardent friends. Possibly he was there himself during this crisis, but he may have left to seek help, to no avail. He may have been urged to leave by those who loved him, as they knew that there could be no mercy if he should be taken. While Glyn Dwr remained free, there was still hope.

After long months of starvation, when the men were weakened and dying from malnutrition and disease, they surrendered, as 1408 drew to an unhappy close. There were no comets to herald 1409, only the cheers of English troops as Harlech was recaptured. Among the prisoners were Glyn Dwr's wife, Margaret, and two of his daughters. Catherine Mortimer's children were taken prisoner, but Edmund had died during the bitter siege. Other brave men of Cymry had died within Harlech's relentless walls; they had preferred to give their lives for a dream of freedom rather than desert the family of their Prince.

It is to the King's credit that he took no revenge on Glyn Dwr's wife, children and grandchildren, who must have given themselves into Talbot's hands expecting harsh treatment. Perhaps they had suffered enough, as the deprivations of Harlech must have left a permanent scar, They were taken to London as prisoners, to be held securely in the capital, far from their homes and beyond the reach of the fugitive Owen Glyn Dwr. The delights of Sycharth and those early years of domestic harmony were fading, poignant memories.

After Harlech had fallen, Glyn Dwr's followers deserted in large numbers, anticipating the end of the struggle. They accepted pardons, paid their fines and returned to their homes to settle down under English rule as if nothing had happened. It was simple enough to deny any involvement, and many were thankful that they had escaped punishment. Prince Henry's policy paid off handsomely. Glyn Dwr and his son, Maredudd, retreated to the mountains and forests, where there was some safety among the few remaining patriots who still refused to surrender. All that remained in Harlech Castle to mark his occupation was a small bronze boss bearing the four lions rampant of Gwynedd. It had fallen unnoticed from a set of horse harness, to lie undiscovered for more than five hundred years.

The Vale of Tywi, boroughs such as Aberteifi, the areas of Gwent, the Gower and Penfro in the South, together with Anglesey and Caernarfon in the North, were all firmly under English control. Outside the boroughs there were still pockets of resistance, particularly in Glamorgan, but they could not withstand the return of English government which gradually reasserted its influence over the defeated populace. Nor could the scattered rebels overcome the antagonism of their countrymen who now wanted peace.

There were faithful friends who remained at Glyn Dwr's side during that terrible time after the fall of Harlech, the symbol of their Cause, and the capture of his family. But the leader's powers of persuasion had failed; his magical, magnetic attraction was diminished. No longer did men flock to his camp or rise at his call for a Free Wales. The confident, upright figure of their Prince had endured too many crippling blows.

One of these more loyal adherents was the Bishop of St Asaph, Trevor, who had formerly supported Henry IV and had been a late convert to the Cause. He had alienated himself from the House of Lancaster and, like his leader, lost everything as a result. In Glyn Dwr's hour of need, Trevor did not desert even though he could have obtained a pardon as many lesser men had done. If he had seen power and glory for himself as a leader of the Church of Wales, when events were more favourable, now there was nothing to gain in the material sense. He stayed with the losing side.

Another bishop who had every intention of joining the Welsh in his capacity as newly-appointed Bishop of Llandaff, was Adam of Usk. In 1407, Pope Benedict XIII confirmed the appointment, at the same time making Gruffydd Young the Bishop of Tyddewi. The French had kept their word on that part of the bargain. Gruffydd Young had served the Welsh Cause in many ways, and the see of Tyddewi would have been his reward. Adam of Usk had been an exile in France, tentatively offering help from a safe distance by corresponding with Northumberland, yet wisely refraining from joining the Earl on his unsuccessful march against Henry. That venture had ended at Bramham Moor; Adam must have thanked his Lord for the sound advice. With the possibility of advancement within the Church of Wales, Adam sailed from Brittany and landed at Abermaw on the Mawddach estuary near Harlech, a small port in the heart of loyalist Wales. His discovery that Glyn Dwr was rapidly losing control prompted him to change his plans, and instead of joining the Welsh he travelled to Y Trallwng to seek the protection of Edward Charlton, Lord of Powys. Like so many others, Adam chose the safe course.

Perhaps it is understandable that those who had more to lose than their lives now crawled to pay homage to King Henry. Those who had sacrificed everything decided that the fight must continue. Philip Hanmer was still loyal; as one of the instigators of the initial uprising he had remained the steadfast brother-in-law. Two brothers, Rhys and Ednyfed of Penmynydd in Anglesey remained true. These two were the sons of Tudur ap Gronw, Glyn Dwr's cousins, who had been active in the campaign from its inception. The other brother, William, who had captured Conwy, was still alive in 1406, but he may have perished in one or other of the later skirmishes. The importance of this Anglesey family becomes apparent after the revolt. The redoubtable Rhys ap Gruffydd, the Black, of Aberteifi, was still prepared to fight. He had abandoned his earlier thoughts of surrender after escaping from Aberystwyth just before it was taken by Prince Henry.

With the remnants of the Welsh army they were now forced to travel the roads of Wales as outlaws, stealing food, attacking poorly-defended settlements for supplies, facing betrayal wherever they went. Their own countrymen were seeking peace with England, and these rebels were upsetting the plans of those who wished to forsake the Cause in return for Henry's forgiveness. They were still a large enough, and wild enough, band to generate alarm among the border townspeople of Oswestry, Ruthin (Clwyd) and Knockin. Every Marcher Lord had been instructed to defend his own territory, but the people of the threatened boroughs prudently obtained a truce from Glyn Dwr to protect their homes and lands from further devastating attacks. This truce may have been the reason for the town of Shrewsbury's reluctance to admit Lord Furnival and his forces, while John was travelling to assist his brother Gilbert Talbot who was scouring North Wales for signs of stray rebels. Throughout 1409, various instructions were sent from London to the Marcher Lords, particularly in the areas of Chirk, Oswestry and Ruthin, to ensure that the outlaws were restrained, and prevented from extracting illegal "truces". Some of the local captains ignored such advice as it was easier to protect their districts by allowing the rebels some leeway. By donating fodder and supplies to the roving Welsh, the bulk of local produce went unharmed. It seems probable that Glyn Dwr had returned to his home-ground, around Sycharth and Carrog. There would still have been enough sympathy, and fear, among the Welsh of those areas to help sustain his diminishing band of followers. There were still family connections to be exploited, and necessity made such connections vital. Large garrisons in the Border strongholds ensured the safety of the castles, but the men and women outside the walls found their own solution. The Welsh rebels were forced to live in this fashion for several months, constantly on the move, wary of their countrymen, robbing former neighbours, desperate for safe refuge as the English troops hounded them from one place to another. John Talbot was just one of the men responsible for driving Glyn Dwr's supporters out of the area, while his brother Gilbert swept Snowdonia clean.

In 1410, a raid along the Shropshire border ended Welsh hopes forever. The constable of Powys castle at Y Trallwng inflicted a crushing defeat on the outlaws. Among the captives were Philip Scudamore of the Herefordshire family; Owen's cousin Rhys ap Tudor of the Conwy Castle venture; and Rhys Ddu of Aberteifi. After torture, and trial as traitors, they were all executed. Scudamore's head was displayed at Shrewsbury as a warning to the border dwellers; Rhys ap Tudor was beheaded at Chester; while the head of Black Rhys was stuck on a pike at London Bridge to prove to the city that the Welsh were defeated. There could be no clemency for these veteran rebels. The town of Y Trallwng was rewarded by Lord Charlton, and in return for unswerving allegiance to the King, the corporation limits were extended.

To add to Glyn Dwr's grief in 1410, a personal blow was the death of Bishop Trevor of St Asaph who had travelled to

France, possibly seeking help for the hopeless Cause. Trevor was buried in Paris, at the Chapel of L'Abbaye de St Victor, having lost everything except his empty title.

From that time, Welsh resistance was reduced to a series of minor disturbances which came to nothing. Glyn Dwr and the remnants of his army were forced to skulk about in the few places where some sympathy still survived. His surviving son, Maredudd, may have accompanied the fugitive warrior as he fled from place to place seeking out those who would help. Perhaps the legends of secret caves and mountain-retreats belong to this sad period in the Prince's tragic life. There were small groups of friends in the Bala district, close to his old home of Carrog in the heart of Merioneth, from where it was easy to escape in many directions. The road to the west led to another group based in the area around Cymmer Abbey, near Dolgellau, where the Nannau lands belonged to Glyn Dwr's family. Although that family connection had been alienated, the estates were large and full of game which could sustain those who sought food. It is a wild and beautiful district where fugitives could hide in relative safety. There were supporters at Strata Florida, north of Tregaron, close to the source of the River Teifi, where many had given their loyalty to the Cause during his successful years. By moving from one hideout to the next, Glyn Dwr was able to evade capture among the mountains and valleys of Mid Wales and the wilderness of Snowdonia.

These "outlaws", no longer patriots, were deeply resented by the vast majority of Welsh people. One result of the constant turbulence was severe taxation. While administrative affairs in Wales had been virtually adjourned for ten years, the payment of rents and taxes, and collection of fines, had been disrupted. King Henry's officers now ensured that people did not escape so lightly, and they were compelled to pay for all the years they had evaded taxation. As the whole country had been affected by large military forces marching from one end to the other, looting and burning, commandeering food and destroying major sources of income, it was very difficult for the inhabitants to find enough money to pay King Henry. It became essential to return to a more settled existence, to rebuild and to re-cultivate, to trade and to restore markets. They wanted to work without fear or interruption in order to satisfy the demands of their masters. The outlaws made this difficult.

They had become accustomed to taking what they required, without payment or argument. They had lost the fight, and people felt that they should now accept the result and leave them to live their lives in peace, if not amity, with the English. Glyn Dwr was given no encouragement, and the men who used his name to excuse their pilfering only brought disgrace to the proud name. He was hard-pressed to remain at liberty and there is little news of his activities other than references to his attempts to find money to survive, In June of 1412 he kidnapped Dafydd Gam, Squint-eyed Davy, of Aberhonddu, demanding a ransom for his prize. It is obvious that the Prince of the Cymry had to resort to banditry to maintain his very existence. There is a story that Gam had infiltrated the Welsh Parliament at Machynlleth, posing as a convert but paid by his master King Henry to assassinate Glyn Dwr.

Gam was a landowner in Aberhonddu who had gained considerable rewards for his loyalty to the crown, and had been granted even more estates after Henry's excursion into Wales in 1401 when Welsh supporters had been punished and disinherited. Of unprepossessing appearance, with his red hair and ungainly figure, long arms and short body, David Gam attended Machynlleth to do homage to Prince Owen. He was a good soldier, and his conversion was welcomed by his fellow Welshmen, but his motives were far from patriotic. Fortunately his murderous intentions were discovered, and his treachery was punished by imprisonment. Glyn Dwr exacted his revenge later by burning Gam's mansion in Aberhonddu. Like many apocryphal tales which gained credence after the revolt, this tale may contain a little truth. Perhaps David Gam did plan to gain himself a title and royal favour by the simple, straightforward murder of Owen Glyn Dwr. The revolt would have crumbled if that one man had died, as the whole insurrection depended on the aura of magical power which encircled the Prince himself. Without their charismatic leader, the patriots could not have fought on as they did.

The story may have arisen after Gam's capture in 1410, as he probably made some effort to escape, and probably attacked his captor. In the ballad, "For Country or For King", the story is perpetuated:

"Come list ye gentles to the tale
That I will tell to you,

Of David Gam, of Brecknock town,
And Vaughan of Ystrad Lliw.

Two kinsmen they of nearest blood,
In steadfast friendship bred,
Till gallant Glyndwr took the field,
And the dragon reared its head.

Now David Gam was for the King,
And for him drew his sword;
But Owen Vaughan was for Glyndwr,
And owned him as his lord."

Gam tries to kill Glyn Dwr as the Welsh meet at their Parliament, but he is prevented by Vaughan. Vaughan asks Glyn Dwr not to kill Gam.

"But David Gam, he loudly cried,
No mercy do I crave;
I came to take thy life away
And not mine own to save.

Thou'st brought a curse upon the land
By thine apostacy;
'Twere better far that Wales should have
Sweet peace than liberty."

Gam was freed, and went on to fight at Agincourt, alongside Henry V. Vaughan remained a patriot, and as Sir Owen Vaughan attempted to assassinate the King during the battle he was thwarted by Gam. David Gam was killed instead, protecting his King, and Vaughan was shot by an archer.

"With his last breath, Vaughan cried out;
His words through Wales yet ring, —
'Tis nobler that a knight should die
For country than for King'."

Both men were buried in one grave. The ballad was written by W. Llewelyn Davies, who expresses the hope that "foul debate" between people and king will now cease. David Gam did die on the field at Agincourt, as did many Welshmen who fought with Henry V.

There were probably other ransoms paid by other captured gentry as the outlaws were driven to desperate measures. Even today hostages are a good source of income for revolutionaries, and when circumstances require unscrupulous methods, those methods are used without conscience or thoughts of dishonour. Glyn Dwr had no alternatives.

Most of his friends were dead; many of his family were dead or disgraced. His son Gruffydd, captured at Usk in 1404, died in the Tower of London, a victim of the plague after six years of imprisonment. He knew that anyone who offered him shelter would be facing great danger, even death. Yet there must have been some faithful and courageous friends.

Disheartened and defeated, Glyn Dwr disappeared. After 1412 no news of the great soldier ever revealed his whereabouts among the mountains of his beloved country. There were opportunists who tried to obtain rewards by disclosing his hiding-places; records reveal that one man was paid one pound in 1413 after he had travelled to London with information against Lord of Glyndyfrdwy. It was a fraudulent claim.

Glyn Dwr's daughter, Catherine Mortimer, died in the autumn of 1413, as did two of her three daughters who had survived the siege of Harlech; the family of Edmund Mortimer was virtually erased.

Friends still worked for the Cause, though they were few and unsuccessful. There is evidence that Philip Hanmer was in France during 1415, accompanied by Owen's former Chancellor, Gruffydd Young, optimistically seeking French aid for the Welsh as France and England prepared for their great wars. Some have suggested that Glyn Dwr himself travelled to France at this time, but his hopes must have been thoroughly dashed by the vicissitudes of these last painful years and the supposition seems most unlikely. The leaders of France had much more important issues to discuss; their country faced invasion. Wales was brushed aside.

Prince Henry succeeded his father on 21st March, 1413. Henry IV of Lancaster had endured a miserable reign of uncertainty and hard fighting, the result of civil war within the kingdom he had hoped to unite. Recognising the magnitude of his sin, Henry had intended to undertake a crusade which was to be atonement for the crime of regicide which he had indirectly committed. His life had been difficult, and harsh; his health had deteriorated rapidly. While he fought his battles, Parliament made life difficult by condemning the endless expense. The Exchequer had grown powerful, and Henry was called to account on more than one occasion. A king no longer had the freedom to be profligate with the nation's money. He was instructed to restrict his household budget and criticised for his poor administration of money, and for his lack of naval defences when the French patrolled the Channel. The inadequate English fleet had allowed the French privateers to plunder towns on the English mainland. The paymasters wanted more for their money and demanded detailed accounts of the king's spending.

There were quarrels with his son and opposition on various matters which resulted in open hostility when Prince Henry queried some of the King's later decisions. In the Prince's opinion, the sick, old man was no longer capable of clear-thinking. Twice during 1412 Prince Henry entered London with a force of men, apparently with the intention of asserting his will backed by military power. Dashing Hal was always willing to go to war with France, while the King sought to preserve peace. Shakespeare portrays Prince Henry as the heir who takes the crown before the King is quite dead; an example of poetic justice.

The King who had stolen a crown could trust no-one, and Prince Henry was determined that no-one else should step in and snatch his inheritance. With good reason the King declares, "Uneasy lies the head that wears a crown." Only in death did he find peace.

Henry V was to become a mighty sovereign, a pious and devout servant of God who established himself as a Christian monarch leading his people to eternal glory. Paradoxically, England's most revered kings won their fame by conquest and war, accompanied by slaughter and bloody triumphs rather than by productive policies and conscientious government. Henry's early training on the battle-fields of England, Scotland and Wales, against such men as Hotspur, and Owen Glyn Dwr, was to culminate in yet greater victories on the soil of France. The exuberant youth, who had enjoyed all the privileges of a soldier's career, was transformed into the King. The carousing and womanising, which were no doubt exaggerated but undeniably part of the youth's life, came to an abrupt halt. There was to be no scandal attached to his person. The snows which accompanied his coronation were interpreted as a sign of the King's purity. He accepted the mantle of responsibility, and preparations for the French campaign began immediately, almost before Henry Bolingbroke's body had been laid to rest.

Henry V needed leaders and soldiers who would subdue England's enemies forever. Many great names had fallen during the reign of his father; many lords had shed their blood for England, many had lost their lands, their families, and their ancient heritage. It was the beginning of a new era. Sons were re-invested with the titles and estates of disgraced fathers. New families were placed in positions of trust. A new generation, descendants of proven loyalists, also surrounded the young King, while those of his father's adherents who still lived served the new master with equal fidelity. A general amnesty was offered to former enemies, the sons of nobles who had served Richard II, such as the young earls of Salisbury, Huntingdon and Oxford. The Earl of March, Mortimer, was freed; the true heir was no longer a threat.

In July, 1415, King Henry V offered a pardon to Owen Glyn Dwr and his remaining colleagues, providing they would offer him their allegiance. The King may have decided that a soldier such as Glyn Dwr would be valuable in his new army. Soldiers develop admiration for their antagonists, and bitter enemies can often respect their adversaries. Gilbert Talbot was authorised to approach the elusive Prince of the Cymry.

Another offer was made in February, 1416, using Glyn Dwr's son Maredudd as intermediary. For some reason there was no reply to either offer. Perhaps he was no longer alive to hear the King's terms. Maredudd received a pardon for himself in April, 1417, which indicates King Henry's good faith. It does not seem that the pardon was merely a trick to force Glyn Dwr into the open. By the standards of his time, Henry V was an honourable man. From his letters, he emerges quite clearly as a generous-natured man who was loyal to friends, and always eager to help those who were in trouble, however minor the occasion of the trouble. The Welsh enemy was defeated; there was no threat to the English throne. There would have been no need to seek a bloody revenge by public humiliation and decapitation of such a gallant gentleman. Henry's generous offer was accepted by many lesser Welsh rebels, who survived the turmoil and retained their lands. One account mentions Henry Don, who had fought alongside Glyn

Dwr in the heyday of Welsh supremacy. The same account names William ap Tudor of Anglesey, the brother of Rhys and Ednyfed who died so tragically at the end of the revolt, but who had not been mentioned after 1406. If Owen's cousin accepted, Owen himself remained silent.

Henry V had other matters to attend to, and Wales was left to subordinates who travelled the countryside to receive submissions. The fractured country was at liberty to heal itself, and many Welshmen decided to erase the painful memories of the past by joining the levies of troops now being gathered for embarkation. France was beckoning.

CHAPTER FOURTEEN

And so, Farewell

"Often the long night he lay alone and companionless,
And did not find in front of him food of his choice;
He had no comrade but his courser in the country wood
and hills,
No traveller to talk to on the track but God,
Till he was nearly nigh to Northern Wales."

Sir Gawain and the Green Knight.

WHERE, and when, Glyn Dwr died remains as much a mystery as the place and date of his birth. The legends began during 1412, suggesting that the great Welsh Prince had melted away by magic into the mountains. Country people believed that he had gone to rest, like King Arthur before him, to sleep peacefully until a resurrection which would free the Welsh people at some time in the future. Many believed that he was a sorcerer with the ability to change his shape and form when danger threatened. Perhaps they saw him as an eagle, or a dragon, safely hidden in his lair among the daunting peaks of Snowdonia where his followers had been most loyal. He may have wandered the hills of Mawddwy, or beckoned from the summit of Cader Idris, the mythical home of Gwynn ap Nudd, Light, Son of the Morning Mist. Nudd, the god of the Britons, had helped Arthur to drive the invaders from his land. Cader Idris was a worthy resting-place for Owen Glyn Dwr until he should be strong enough to return to his people. Or did the solitary Prince roam the heights of Plynlimon, hearing again the ghostly war-cries of his jubilant followers as they carried his standard into battle, to victory.

On a less exalted and less fanciful level, it is possible that he sought the safety of his daughter's house in Herefordshire. Alice had married John Scudamore of that county, before the revolt. One of his manors was at Monnington Straddel in the Golden Valley, and Glyn Dwr may have found sanctuary in that peaceful country haven. Worn out by years of hardship and hunger, of grief and failure, the warrior may have found comfort and love to ease his bitter pain. His wars had not involved Alice, although as in many families, loyalties had been divided. Philip Scudamore had been executed as a traitor, but John Scudamore was a King's man. If Alice's home in Herefordshire were his last resting-place, those gentle green slopes would have ensured an undisturbed site for the body of an outlawed Prince. A place to die would have been Alice's only contribution to the lost Cause so dear to her father. For safety's sake he would have been buried without ceremony, without a stone to mark his grave, without publicity which could have harmed the Scudamore family even though an amnesty had been offered. The idea of such a grave appeals to those who would seek a pleasant finale.

It would not have been a happy sanctuary for Glyn Dwr. Across the River Monnow, Grosmont would have been a grim reminder of the most tragic battle in his weary campaign. If only Rhys Gethin had not been so headstrong; if only the Welsh had restricted themselves to the type of warfare they knew best; if only Prince Henry had been captured at Grosmont, if only . . .

It is hard to believe that Owen, Prince of Wales, chose this alien haven for his burial-place, outside the country he loved, far from friends and tended by an Anglicised daughter. Yet the sheer physical effort required for twelve years' hard campaigning must have taken a dreadful toll. He was more than fifty years old. Wales is a hard country, and Glyn Dwr had traversed every mile, many times, in all seasons. No man could have done more.

Folk-memory recalls a more solitary end, as cold and bitter as the last futile months of his campaign. It is said that he died in the mountains, accompanied only by a faithful friend. There on a bleak summit he was interred in a cave, protected by boulders; a secret place where no-one could ever disturb his rest. His name was kept alive by the bards of later generations, revered and honoured as Wales' last great patriot.

The fickleness of Fortune, described so poignantly in the original story of Arthur, ensured that the hero's success, on Earth, was only fleeting. Like Arthur, Owen had sought to rule a kingdom, but his heroic struggles had caused suffering and destruction. His friends had been killed; his family estranged, captured or dead. He too, was broken on the Wheel of Fortune, and forced to walk alone. The *Morte Arthure*, an anonymous alliterative poem of Glyn Dwr's own times, mirrored his own fate.

He had inspired loyalty and courage. He had lost everything dear to him, trying to free his countrymen from the iron fist of England. The country gentleman had become an inspiring military leader, a Prince of his people and a hunted outlaw. Such men are few. His sacrifice was without reservation.

"In a winter's dream, on Gamelyn Moor,
I found the lost grave of the Lord Glyndwr.
Three shadows I followed against the moon,
That marched while the grey reeds whistled the tune.
Three swordsmen they were, out of Harry's wars,
That made a Welsh song of their Norman scars.
But they sang no longer of Agincourt,
When they came to a grave; for there lay Glyndwr.
Straightway I saw the dead forth-stand,
His good sword bright in his right hand.
. . . .
Oh, bright it shines, and shall brighter gleam,
For all that believe in the Cymric dream."
The Ballad of the Buried Sword — Ernest Rhys

It was a brief episode in British history. The people of Wales would see more battles, more besieged castles and trampling armies, and more hardship. Never again would they see such a patriot. England, and the new English language, would go on to become conquerors of a new world as Wales became part of the scheme instead of achieving a separate identity.

History would label Glyn Dwr a rebel, a greedy upstart whose cruelty and ambition harmed both England and Wales. He had dared to oppose the might of the Lancasters. He had been a traitor, to England, and many had died or been ruined by the "Welsh Episode" of 1400. Yet he had fought for a belief, a freedom, a country; he had almost succeeded in uniting the Welsh people if only for a few years. It was his misfortune that his attempt coincided with the rise of the House of Lancaster. Henry V went on to win victories such as Agincourt, to defeat France, and to ensure that his name lives on in history as the greatest military sovereign of all time. He had sharpened his sword on the enemies within his own kingdom; the dress-rehearsal had been staged in Wales

Glyn Dwr could not compete, partly because of the half-hearted response from men of his own class, the lack of skilled soldiers, and because patriotism did not feed empty bellies. His soldiers were mostly peasants and farmers, hot-headed students and a selection of vagabonds, led by headstrong captains who had no knowledge of tactics. They were eager to attack by stealth but unwilling, and incapable, of meeting the disciplined, trained English soldiers face to face.

The men from the North did not mix easily with the men from the South. Loyalties were fickle, and it was difficult trying to sustain hostilities with men who were not certain that their leader was capable of beating the enemy led by such men as Prince Henry and the great Marcher Lords who accompanied him. The Welsh lacked noble leaders to help Glyn Dwr. Their Prince could rally faint hearts by a personal appearance, but he could not divide his person to maintain unswerving allegiance throughout his scattered forces. Too many were too willing to betray him. It is a sad thought that land-owners were so eager to pay a fine to King Henry that they gained their farms, but lost a country.

It should also be remembered that Wales was not the clearly-defined country that exists today. Many Welshmen fought on the side of the English because their homes were in English territory. Glyn Dwr's support came from the Old Wales, a much smaller area than the twentieth century Principality, with the former counties of Caernarfonshire and Merionethshire, then as now Gwynedd, as the heartland. Today, Gwynedd, and the western county of Dyfed, where Glyn Dwr also found support, lead the country in their efforts to preserve the language and culture of Wales. Traditions have survived.

Wales could not recover from the devastation. The people suffered for many years as they struggled to live under English domination, paying rents and taxes, trying to restore their ruined towns and farms, re-building prosperity.

Many outlaws continued to live by terrorising and stealing, roaming the countryside in their search for food and a safe hiding-place. It had become a way of life. There were those who blamed Glyn Dwr. They blamed him for their lost wealth, their dead sons and brothers, their loss of comfort during the rebellion. His main strength had been drawn from the lower classes, and they ensured that his name lived on through legend, poem and romance. To the English he would be "that Welsh traitor"; to the people of Wales he remained a Prince, unsuccessful this time but a Prince who would return one day, to free them from their hated masters. Perhaps in death, Owen Glyn Dwr gained more glory than he had attracted during his brief reign. If all the glowing tributes and retrospective praise could have been utilised the story would have been very different. During the centuries which followed, the gulf between the Welsh gentry and the lower classes widened into a chasm, although respect for a man's ancestors is still as strong today, with the result that a manual worker can claim kinship with the family of his landlord, and often does. The wealthier Welsh benefitted from the English connection, and, to some extent, the poorer classes gained from the union. But the English should not despise, or belittle, Owen Glyn Dwr.

"There is a history in all men's lives
Figuring the nature of the times deceased;
The which observed, a man may prophesy,
With a near aim, of the main chance of things
As yet not come to life, which in their seeds
And weak beginnings lie intreasured.
Such things become the hatch and brood of time . . . "

Henry IV, Part One.
Act III scene i.

CHAPTER FIFTEEN

The Welsh King

"Courageous Richmond, well hast thou acquit thee!
Lo, here, this long-usurped royalty
From the dead temples of this bloody wretch
Have I pluck'd off, to grace thy brows withal:
Wear it, enjoy it, and make much of it."

William Shakespeare.
Richard III
Act V scene v.

HENRY V possessed remarkable powers of leadership. His abilities as a military genius were recognised by the thousands of soldiers who gave their lives in his name. After the unprofitable conflicts within Britain, captains were eager to set sail for France where there were fortunes to be made by ambitious men. New honours and wealth awaited the victors. Shakespeare's Henry V called on his men to fight for "Harry, England and Saint George", but the real reasons for such endeavours were more mercenary than noble.

From the beginning of his reign, Henry planned to invade France. As Prince of Wales he had failed to stir his war-weary father into declaring open hostilities, but now the crown was his he did not hesitate. The army that sailed the Channel in 1415 consisted of all the great English lords of an aggressive country, united in his service. Among them were his brothers, the Duke of Clarence and the Duke of Gloucester. Former enemies now joined their King, reinstated to their former positions with their estates intact. Mortimer, the Earl of March, who had now grown up and was no longer a threat to the King, served Henry loyally in France. The Duke of York, his cousin, died in France, although York's brother, the Earl of Cambridge, had attempted to dethrone Henry during 1415 and suffered a traitor's death. The expedition of 1417 also saw the new Earl of Northumberland accompanying King Henry, having been restored to his grandfather's lands and titles in

1416. It seems that Henry bore no grudges; he certainly anticipated no further rebellions as he led his people into war.

The wars in France, generally referred to as the Hundred Years' War which lasted intermittently from 1361 until 1453, brought great glory to England and rich territories to be ruled by the English throne. There were many battles and arduous campaigns, the most famous being the Battle of Agincourt, which were to become a difficult inheritance for the next monarch. Henry's army consisted of men from England, Scotland and Wales; enmities had been forgotten in such a short time. The Fluellen of Shakespeare's *Henry V* was a loyal and trusted Welsh soldier whose military ability was unquestionable. The success of the English army was largely due to the archers' skill with the Welsh longbow, that lethal and devastating weapon which had been adopted and encouraged by Richard II. The invaders suffered from disease, as sickness spread rapidly through the ranks, but the more unpleasant side of the medieval warfare is forgotten in the euphoria of English victory. Harfleur and Agincourt are names to conjure up visions of proud knights and Henry's courage against incredible odds as they hacked the French to pieces. There were long sieges where Henry's past experience proved essential, experience he had gained in Wales when he stormed Aberystwyth. The battles in France were, however, fought in traditional fashion, on the open field; Henry V proved himself to be a truly magnificent leader, handsome, brave and victorious.

Henry V married Catherine, the daughter of Charles VI, to consolidate his claim to the French throne. His military prowess had subdued a large part of northern France but he sought control of a much larger portion, and this could be accomplished more easily by arrangement before the altar than by besieging obstinate towns. At the age of thirty-five, after a brief and glorious reign, Henry V died in 1422, leaving a nine-month old son as heir to the throne. After a long minority, during which England's affairs were managed by the powerful nobles, Henry VI faced the difficult task of retaining French conquests across the Channel.

In 1445, Henry VI married Margaret of Anjou, daughter of the French King Charles VII. There was an uneasy truce between the warring countries until Charles was able to overcome the English presence throughout his country. By

1453, England had lost every acre of France except the town of Calais. The kingdoms were now completely separated and the descendants of William the Conqueror had to forgo their claims to lands in Normandy, Aquitaine, and a claim to the French throne which had been acknowledged for centuries.

Henry VI was a very different man to the hypnotic and commanding leader exemplified by his father. A council of churchmen and ministers had ruled England until he grew up, which left the country's affairs in the hands of ambitious families. In later years, Margaret of Anjou, Henry's wife, attempted to become the driving-force while the King suffered long periods of insanity. The Earls who had wielded so much power during Henry's minority saw an opportunity to gain absolute power, rather than let French Margaret assert herself as Queen. They began to quarrel amongst themselves for the tempting prize. The Wars of the Roses had begun.

The rule of the House of Lancaster had originated with Henry IV, followed by Henry V, Henry VI, and in succession the heir to the sick monarch, Edward, Prince of Wales.

A parallel claim developed as a result of the earlier Lancaster rebellion of 1399. At the death of Richard II, the legitimate heir was Edmund Mortimer, the boy Earl of March whose father, Roger, had died in Ireland in 1398 on Richard's campaign. This boy was kept under guard by Henry IV to prevent anyone from raising a revolt in the Mortimer name. The Earl's uncle Edmund had married the daughter of Glyn Dwr and died during the siege of Harlech Castle. The Earl of March apparently did not entertain any royal ambitions, excepting minor incidents when he was used as a tool by others, and he fought with Henry V in France. He was no danger to the throne and those who sought to place him there were executed. Anne Mortimer, however, the Earl's sister, married Richard the Earl of Cambridge who was yet another descendant of Edward III. Richard's father was the Duke of York, fifth son of mighty Edward and Philippa. The union of Mortimer and Cambridge produced a son, Richard, who adopted the title Duke of York after his father's brother, the Duke, died at Agincourt. He took the surname of Plantagenet. The Earl of Cambridge was executed by Henry V after he had tried to organise a rebellion in the name of Mortimer. As the struggle for the crown developed, the Duke of York tried to establish his family's right to the throne by the force of arms.

He saw no reason why a mad king, a Lancaster, and a French Queen, should rule England while the true heirs were displaced. The Duke was killed at the Battle of Wakefield, near Sandal Castle, in 1460. The Yorkist party gained supremacy, and after Henry VI and Queen Margaret had been forced to flee to Scotland for safety, York's son was declared King Edward IV in 1461. His brothers were George, the Duke of Clarence, and Richard Duke of Gloucester.

Intrigue and ambition are woven through this period of bloody history as civil war tore England apart. Edward IV held on to his throne and mad Henry VI died a prisoner in the Tower of London. The Lancaster heir, Edward, son of Henry and Margaret of Anjou, was killed at the Battle of Tewkesbury in 1471. The dynasty begun by Henry Bolingbroke ended as it had begun, on the battlefield.

When King Edward died in 1483, the Yorkist heir Edward V was only twelve years old. He and his brother Richard have achieved unenviable fame as the Princes in the Tower. The boy King reigned for only a few months until a more experienced hand snatched the crown. The Princes, or rather the King and his brother, disappeared. George the Duke of Clarence, their uncle, had already been eliminated, drowned in a butt of malmsey wine if we are to believe the legend; uncle Edmund, the Earl of Rutland, had been killed at the Battle of Wakefield with his father the Duke in 1460. Only uncle Richard remained; the Duke of Gloucester who was to become the Hunchback King Richard III.

The events of these cruel years of murder, sudden death and disappearances brought inevitable decline to the House of Plantagenet. Richard sought to establish a new family by marrying Anne, the widow of Henry VI's son who had died at Tewkesbury. It was a logical step by which Richard hoped to end the Wars. But Richard's accession was the signal for yet another claimant who had been waiting in the wings, supported by those who hated the Yorkist faction, and the new King whose dubious methods had achieved such drastic results.

Springing from that same John of Gaunt who had produced Henry IV, came the House of Beaufort, the children of John's third marriage to Katherine Swynford. Although the daughter of a gentleman, Katherine's origins were comparatively low and she served in the Gaunt household as a governess. Her sister Philippa had married Geoffrey Chaucer, but she had been compelled to marry a poor knight, Sir Hugh Swynford, as an alternative to entering a convent. By working under the protection of John of Gaunt and his wife Blanche, Katherine had survived an obscure fate to become John's mistress. The attractive widow Swynford produced healthy children, who grew up alongside the Lancaster offspring. Their legitimacy had been confirmed and legalised by charter during the reign of Richard II, after John of Gaunt caused a great scandal by marrying his mistress. During each successive reign the Beaufort family had grown increasingly powerful, serving each monarch as military commanders or eminent churchmen, acquiring new titles and riches. John Beaufort became Earl of Somerset; Henry became Bishop of Winchester and a Cardinal, and served as Chancellor of the realm until he died in 1447. Thomas became Duke of Exeter, while Joan married into the great Westmoreland family of Neville. The Wars of the Roses took their toll of the Beaufort family, virtually destroying the male line, so that the heiress of the senior line was Lady Margaret Beaufort, John of Gaunt's great grand-daughter.

When Henry V died, still a young man, he left a young widow, daughter of the Valois kings of France. Catherine's baby son had become Henry VI. This former Queen married again, not to an English noble as one might have expected, but to Owen Tudor, a son of the royal line of Wales. His descent could be traced from Ednyfed Fychan of Anglesey, a minister in the council of Llywelyn the Great. Ednyfed in turn was descended from Rhodri Mawr and King Hywel Dda, through the House of Lord Rhys the master of Deheubarth. Ironically, this family from Penmynydd was that same family which had provided Owen Glyn Dwr with his two memorable captains, William and Rhys. These Anglesey cousins had another brother, Meredith, who succeeded to the title and estates and produced a son, Owen Tudor, to win the heart of Catherine Valois. While Fate had watched Glyn Dwr wage an unequal battle against the future Henry V, and smilingly observed the Lord of Glyndyfrdwy's family lose their homes and fortunes, it was Henry V's widow who was destined to marry Glyn Dwr's relative.

The son of this marriage was Edmund Tudor, Earl of Richmond. Edmund married the Beaufort heiress, Margaret, and the child of this powerful family was known as Henry Tudor, or Henry of Richmond. He fought at the Battle of

Tewkesbury in 1471, as a Lancastrian supporter, but after the Prince of Wales had been killed he was forced to flee to the safety of Brittany, leaving England to the mercies of Richard the Hunchback. The Beauforts naturally fought for the Lancastrian King and their lives were not safe once the Yorkist assumed control.

As a descendant of the royal House of Lancaster, and the son of a line of Welsh Princes, however indistinct, Henry's claim to the throne of England was supported by many rich and powerful families of England and Wales. In 1485, assisted by his uncle Jasper, Earl of Pembroke, Henry left the shores of France with a small band of followers determined to overthrow the Yorkist King. It is said that he intended to land at Abermaw on the Mawddach estuary where loyal supporters waited in Ardudwy under the command of the Vaughan family who lived at Cors y Gedol in Dyffryn. There had been strong Lancastrian loyalties in that area for many years, and the small port was well-known to Brittany seamen. However, driven by gales to find safe harbour, Henry's ships landed at Milffwrd, further south on the Welsh coast. Men flocked to his side as they headed for England through Aberteifi, Machynlleth, Y Trallwng, and on to Stafford. On 22nd August they reached Bosworth, near Atherstone. In this famous battle, Richard III was defeated and killed, leaving the crown to Henry Tudor and the Lancastrians;

"God and your arms be praised, victorious friends,
The day is ours, the bloody dog is dead."

Richard III
Act V scene v.

Henry VII was primarily responsible for restoring peace and order to a land ravaged by civil war. His reign was not easy; he too had to contend with other claimants who appeared at intervals to claim the crown. He had to restore prosperity to a country riven by the Wars of the Roses, which he did by hard management and a strong grasp of financial matters. He was prudent, unemotional, and a stabilising influence at a crucial time in England's history. Any fiery blood in his veins had been tempered by transfusion, and when he chose as his bride the heiress of the House of York, Elizabeth, the great Houses were truly united. Elizabeth had survived the murder of her brothers, and the blood of Edward III continued to flow in her veins to give England an English Queen.

> *"Oh now, let Richmond and Elizabeth,*
> *The true succeeders of each royal house,*
> *By God's fair ordinance conjoin together . . . "*

The Red and the White Roses were, at last, grafted on the same tree and their son Henry was to add his exploits to English history as the magnificent, much-married Henry VIII.

From the time of the Glyn Dwr rebellion of 1400, only eighty-five years elapsed before a Welsh King obtained the throne of England by hereditary claim. The years between were years of conflict, war and death both at home and abroad. The people endured hardships and cruelty, inevitable victims as one lord fought another in the great struggle for power.

In Wales, the people obeyed their rulers, dying for causes they barely understood. When, at last, Henry Tudor appeared on the scene as a contestant, the Welsh nobility and Welsh farmers were quite willing to support this son of Lancaster, who happened to be a son of Wales. Where men had fought for Richard against the usurper Henry, they now adjusted their loyalty to match the destiny of a Lancastrian Tudor. When we consider the events of the past eighty-five years, such shifting loyalties and new alliances are not unusual. Britain is now allied against former allies and friends on a much larger scale in a kaleidoscopic arena.

There is a story that Glyn Dwr was walking on the hills near Llangollen, when he met the abbott of Valle Crucis. He joked with the abbott, commenting that the good man had risen early. The reply was, "No, it is you have risen too early. A hundred years before your time."

Perhaps Glyn Dwr would have had a great impact on events towards the end of the fifteenth century, as a military commander helping Henry Tudor to the throne. There is, indeed, an eerie resemblance between Glyn Dwr and Macchiavelli's Prince of the following century. Although the Prince of the Cymry was not successful, some of his methods were exactly those recommended in *Il Principe,* and the reactions of some of his more fickle followers were those described so cynically by the Italian;

"They would shed their blood for you, risk their property, their lives, their children, so long, as I said above, danger is remote; but when you are in danger, they turn against you."

Il Principe, Chapter XVII

By the time Henry VII had established himself, the affairs of England and Wales were more the affairs of Britain as a nation. Glyn Dwr's effect on affairs in his own time was, for a brief and hectic period, the effect of a great patriot leading his conquered people in a very unequal struggle. While English historians blackened his name, and the Welsh people settled down to their lives under English dominance, Glyn Dwr's name lived on in many sympathetic hearts. Their hero's exploits were passed on in folk-tale and song, from generation to generation. Had they shown as much admiration when he was alive, the story might have been different. He gave everything he had for his dream, a sacrifice which is not demanded of, or given, by many. He is remembered for this, and his failure becomes irrevelant.

Most history books apportion a page, or a paragraph, to the uprising of Owen Glyn Dwr. His struggle was overshadowed by the glorious deeds and foreign conquests of Henry V, or it became a subsidiary episode, lost among the intricate affairs of feuding families headed by English earls such as Northumberland. Unlike Scotland, Wales did not produce a separate line of kings to punctuate the pages of the past. Henry VII's Welsh connection is glossed over, and the emphasis placed on the Lancaster-Beaufort inheritance. Dowager Queen Catherine's secret love for the courtier Owen Tudor, and her subsequent marriage to the young Welshman, had not been acceptable and was, for a time, illegal. Owen was imprisoned and the two lovers separated after a law was passed to forbid such a marriage, if, indeed, it ever took place. Catherine died in January, 1437. She was buried in the Lady Chapel of Westminster Abbey, but when Henry VII instigated alterations to the Lady Chapel her corpse was exhumed and casually placed beside the tomb of Henry V. As the remains were loosely wrapped in lead, the bizarre outcome of this undignified "burial" was a Queen's corpse on public exhibition. Anyone who wished was able to view, and touch, her mouldering remains. Some said that this abasement was the voluntary penance of a conscience-stricken Queen, the wife, and mother, of kings who had consorted with a commoner against the ruling of church and state. The diarist Samuel Pepys indulged in this macabre pastime in 1669, to celebrate his birthday, when he both touched and kissed poor Catherine's corpse. It was not until the eighteenth century that she was, at last, laid to rest, and placed beyond the reach of curious hands, and lips.

The Tudor dynasty was to last for nearly one hundred and twenty years and was represented finally by that most English queen, Elizabeth I. Catherine's children were declared legitimate and granted suitable titles, with the result that Edmund was able to marry Margaret Beaufort, and Jasper became the Earl of Pembroke, the man responsible for ensuring that Edmund's son, Henry of Richmond, survived the Wars of the Roses to become King.

Scotland provided a King for a united kingdom, when James I succeeded Elizabeth I, and Wales had already become the western part of England as far as legislation and Government were concerned.

Henry VIII's reign had seen the 1535 Act of Parliament which ended the unjust system of Marcher Lordships, an inheritance from the Norman invasion which had been the prime cause of resentment for centuries. The Act of Union was in response to the requests and petitions of the Welsh, who rightly felt that there was discrimination. During Elizabeth's reign, the gentry of Wales derived great benefits from the Union and many established themselves in important positions at court. Welshmen were able to make their names, and fortunes, during the prosperous years of Queen Bess.

Centuries of colonisation, contact with English ideas and fashions, and the lure of opportunities in England, almost obliterated the identity of the Welsh people. But just as the translation of the Bible into English had stimulated the growth of that language, the Welsh Bible saved the old tongue for Wales. While the upper classes assimilated English modes and adopted the English language, the lower classes continued to use the British tongue in their daily lives. Just as Glyn Dwr's main support had come from the people, Welsh identity was preserved through the ensuing centuries by the ordinary people.

Today, the struggle has been renewed, and the emphasis has

been placed on the retention of the Welsh language and the resurrection of Welsh culture. It will be a war of words not swords. Wales has produced some exceptional orators, and, as in Glyn Dwr's revolt, the impetus comes from students, churchmen, and the people.

Visitors to Wales might be forgiven for regarding Welsh culture as quaint, even prehistoric, in an age when most countries are pushing forwards, not backwards. To an English ear, the strange sounds of "penillion" seem almost discordant, as singer and harpist hurry along separate routes to reach their final destination, each apparently following his own inclinations. Welsh poetry often seems too strictly fashioned, limited to set patterns, when compared to the essential freedom of English verse. Clog-dancers are not regarded with the same tolerance as Morris Dancers, and performers at the Medieval Banquets, which are now tourist attractions, too often become caricatures. The culture paraded for visitors is not comparable to the spontaneous and unrehearsed community Noson Lawen or Social Night. Shakespeare's Fluellen has much to answer for, as "Look you" is not the language of the Welshman. The great wealth of English culture and tradition tends to obscure the achievements of the Welsh unless, like Dylan Thomas, they write in English and become universally recognised. While the techniques of Welsh poetry are lost in translation, the emotional beauty can still be appreciated. It is a country to stir the soul, and many poets have sprung from the farms and hillside cottages where men are closest to nature. The verses breathe with a vivid freshness which can only spring from a heart that loves the country. The farmer has as much opportunity to win the bardic chair as his university-educated cousin, and the pre-occupation with poetry and music is as strong today as it was a thousand years ago.

The present Prince of Wales was invested at Caernarfon Castle in 1969, a tradition begun by Edward I in 1301. His descent can be traced from the royal houses of England, Scotland, Ireland and Wales. Henry Tudor represented the princes of South Wales, and his queen, Elizabeth of York, represented the princes of North Wales. Both were descended from Rhodri Mawr, the ninth century ruler of independent Wales.

We must hope that the heroes who will arise in the twentieth century to establish Wales as a separate country will adopt more civilised attitudes and methods than those of Glyn Dwr and his followers. The Lord of Glyndyfrdwy would certainly have used legal procedure had it been as powerful as it is today. Parliament failed him, and a rebel leader was born. The Welsh people have remained a separate race, in spite of amalgamation and English influence over centuries. In the Referendum of 1979, which took place appropriately enough on St David's Day, 1st March, the people rejected plans for an Assembly. The highest percentage of voters in favour of the proposal to establish a House of Representatives in Cardiff was 22.46 per cent in Gwynedd; Owen Glyn Dwr's kingdom has changed considerably since 1400, but at least Welsh Gwynedd was more true to his Cause than other counties.

The financial situation in 1979 had a great effect on the views of voters when they were offered an Assembly to run their own affairs in Wales. It is interesting that finance, or the lack of it, hampered Henry IV to such an extent that Wales was able to win temporary independence in the fifteenth century. Today it has become virtually impossible to separate Wales from England because of financial entanglement. No amount of patriotic fervour can allay the fears of taxpayers and much of the discussion which preceded the Referendum reflected this fear. The campaign also revived old jealousies between North and South, with the result that many residents in Gwynedd could see no reason for basing an Assembly in Caerdydd when Caernarfon, or Machynlleth, is a more appropriate centre for Welsh affairs.

The people's decision in 1979 does not mean that the matter is settled. There were many who voted "No", or abstained, because the terms of the proposal were unacceptable, or too vague. The Welsh language faces an uphill struggle in a world where communication must be simplified to maintain peaceful co-existence. But there are many who will persevere, using education as the weapon. The engulfing tide of uniformity will not drown the voice of Wales, and the language attracts support from some unexpected allies. As English settlers continue to choose Wales for their permanent homes, their children are taught in Welsh schools where they learn both the language and the history of Wales. Some of the most vehement advocates of the twentieth century Cause are those who have grown to admire and respect the wild country of the Britons. This assimilation is not a new phenomenon, as a glance at the names of Glyn Dwr's supporters will verify. Many countries are bi-lingual and operate successfully without any antagonism. It is easy to condemn those who use direct, often illegal, means to publicise their beliefs. For the English, who too often regard Wales as their recreational playground, a place where cottages are cheap and beautifully situated, the antics of Nationalists are merely an inconvenience to be tolerated. Perhaps the English grew accustomed to controlling other countries, and failed to appreciate that the "natives" might not welcome the obliteration of their heritage. The current invasion does not consist of armed knights and bold archers, but of boot-clad climbers, caravanners and tourists. Many visitors are tempted to buy homes in this unspoilt country, and many dilapidated buildings have been restored by imaginative owners who seek the peace and solitude of life in the countryside. Yet they fail to understand the anger and the resentment that their actions arouse as villages and towns die a slow death. Commuters, drawn to Wales by the irresistible lure of sea and mountains, forests and green fields, are thoughtlessly destroying what they sought to preserve. The solution is not simple, and Wales, like parts of England itself, is not the only place to suffer strangulation by second-homes. It is paradoxical that the natural assets of Wales may prove to be as disastrous to the inhabitants as the conquering armies of Edward I and Henry IV. Snowdonia (Eryri) was once invincible; now the trampling feet of tourists are wearing away the summit of the mountain, although it claims many sacrificial victims as compensation.

The Welsh Language Society will continue the campaign to establish an ancient identity, and if Glyn Dwr lies sleeping there are many waiting to follow his banner. Individuality, freedom, and independence are still words to arouse a nation. The red dragon still stalks the uplands of Plynlimon, temporarily defeated, but determined to survive. By learning something of the history of this proud country we may understand why this dragon is immortal, and why it should survive.

Strong son of Wales! thy fate
Not without tears, our Cymric memories keep;
Our faithful, unforgetting natures weep
The ancestral fallen Great.
Not with the stalwart arm, nor the keen uplifted sword,
But with the written or the spoken word

Would fain her power increase;
The Light we strive to spread
Is Knowledge, and its power
Comes not from captured town or leagured tower.
A closer brotherhood
Unites the Cymric and the Anglian blood,
Yet separate, side by side, they dwell, not one,
Distinct till Time be done."

Sir Lewis Morris
Poems of Wales 1914.

APPENDIX I

Place Names and Details of Counties

1) Places in the book where the name is the same in English and Welsh.

Aberffraw
Abergavenny
Abergynolwyn
Aberystwyth
Archenfield
Ardudwy

Bala
Bangor
Beaumaris
Beddgelert
Betws-y-coed
Bridgend
Bryn Glas

Cader Idris
Caerleon
Caernarfon
Caerphilly
Carreg Cennen
Carrog
Carrogin Gwynedd
Ceiriog
Ceredigion
Chirk
Cilgerran
Coity
Conwy
Craig-y-Dorth
Criccieth
Cwm Hir
Cymmer
Cynllaith

Defynnog
Denbigh
Derwen
Dinas Powis
Dinefwr
Dolbadarn
Dolgellau
Dolwyddelan
Dryslwyn
Dyffryn

Eifionydd

Flint
Foxall

Ganllwyd
Glyndyfrdwy
Gower
Grosmont
Gwynionydd

Harlech
Hawarden
Hay-on-Wye
Holt
Hyddgen

Iscoed

Kidwelly

Laugharne
Llanbadarn-fawr
Llanberis
Llandaff
Llandeilo
Llandrindod Wells
Llanegryn
Llanelltyd
Llanfaes
Llanfair Dyffryn Clwyd
Llangollen
Llansilin
Llanstephan
Lleyn

Machynlleth
Maelienydd
Mawddwy
Montgomery

Nannau
Nant y moch
New Radnor

Ogmore

Penmorfa
Penmynydd
Pennal
Pilleth
Presteigne

Radnor
Rhuddlan
Ruthin

Strata Florida
St Asaph

Talgarth
Tintern
Treffgarne
Trefgarn Owain
Tregaron
Tywyn

Usk

Valle Crucis

2) Welsh/English and English/Welsh place name in the book.

Welsh	*English*	*English*	*Welsh*
Aberdyfi	Aberdovey	Aberdovey	Aberdyfi
Aberhonddu	Brecon	Barmouth	Abermaw
Abermaw	Barmouth	Brecon	Aberhonddu
Abertawe	Swansea	Builth Wells	Llanfair-ym-Muallt
Aberteifi	Cardigan	Cardiff	Caerdydd

Caerdydd	Cardiff	Cardigan	Aberteifi
Caerfyrddin	Carmarthen	Carmarthen	Caerfyrddin
Casnewydd	Newport	Cilmery	Cilmeri
Castell Newydd Emlyn	Newcastle Emlyn	Haverfordwest	Hwiffordd
Cilmeri	Cilmery	Knighton	Tref-y-Clawdd
Dinbych y Pysgod	Tenby	Llandovery	Llanymddyfri
Hwiffordd	Haverfordwest	Llanfachreth	Llanfachraeth
Llanfachraeth	Llanfachreth	Milford Haven	Milffwrd
Llanfair-ym-Muallt	Builth Wells	Monmouth	Trefynwy
Llanymddyfri	Llandovery	Newcastle Emlyn	Castell Newydd Emlyn
Milffwrd	Milford Haven	Newport	Casnewydd
Penfro	Pembroke	Pembroke	Penfro
San Cler	St Clears	St Clears	San Cler
Tref-y-Clawdd	Knighton	St David's	Tyddewi
Trefynwy	Monmouth	Swansea	Abertawe
Tyddewi	St David's	Tenby	Dinbych y Pasgod
Y Trallwng	Welshpool	Welshpool	Y Trallwng

3) Counties. In April 1974 thirteen counties amalgamated to form eight new and larger counties.

Anglesey, Caernarfonshire, Merioneth } became Gwynedd

Flintshire, Denbighshire } became Clwyd

Brecknock, Montgomeryshire, Radnorshire } became Powys

Cardiganshire, Carmarthenshire, Pembrokeshire } became Dyfed

Monmouthshire became Gwent

Glamorgan split to become West Glamorgan, Mid Glamorgan, South Glamorgan

APPENDIX II

Castles and Places Connected with Glyn Dwr

It would be impossible to list all the castles and other places of interest which are mentioned in the text or which are linked in some way to the story of Glyn Dwr. The following are some such places to visit or to study by further reading. The Wales Tourist Board publish excellent guides which are inexpensive and invaluable when touring in Wales. Place names set in bold type indicate location and where English name varies from the Welsh it follows in brackets.

Abergavenny Castle, South East Wales. In 1176 the Norman knight William de Braose invited the Welsh lords as guests but the men of Gwent were murdered as they sat at table. In 1403 Glyn Dwr burned the town.

Aberhonddu (Brecon) Castle, Mid Wales Borderlands. Built by William I's half-brother. Attacked by Welsh forces in 1403. Probable residence for plan of marriage between Henry VII and Elizabeth, daughter of Edward IV.

Aberteifi (Cardigan) Castle, West Wales. Famous for an early Eisteddfod in 1176 which was organised by the Lord Rhys, Prince of South Wales.

Aberystwyth Castle, Mid Wales. Original castle of Llanfarian on site further south. Edward I built present castle which was captured by Glyn Dwr in 1404 and recaptured by Prince Henry in 1408.

Battlefield Church, near **Shrewsbury**, Salop. Built on the orders of Henry IV on the Whitchurch Road to mark the site of the Battle on 22nd July, 1403. The shields on the hammer-beams inside are the coats-of-arms of knights who took part in the battle. On the north side those of Henry IV, Earl of Dunbar, Sir Hugh Stanley, Sir John Cockayne, Sir Nicholas Gausel, Sir Hugh Mortimer, Sir Hugh Sirley, Sir Robert Malveysin, Sir Madoc Kynaston, Sir Richard Sandford, Sir Francis Bromley and Sir Edward de Rowson. On the south side those of Henry, Prince of Wales, Earl of Stafford, Sir John Clifton, Sir Walter Blout, Sir Robert Gausel, Sir John Massey, Sir Thomas Wendesley, Sir Reginald Mottershed, Sir Jenkin Hanmer and Sir Richard Hussey.

Beaumaris Castle, North West Wales. Edward I's last great castle. Totally secure and impregnable. Easily held by small garrison.

Caerdydd (Cardiff) Castle, South Wales. Roman site, twelfth century keep. In 1404 Glyn Dwr caused destruction in the town and damaged parts of the castle defences later in his campaign.

Caerfyrddin (Carmarthen) Castle, South West Wales. Captured in 1403 by Glyn Dwr and lost again. French help in 1405 placed town under Welsh control again for a short period. Originally Roman fort and settlement of Moridunum.

Caernarfon Castle, North West Wales. An Edward I castle closely associated with the Prince of Wales since 1301 and on the site of an earlier William I castle. Roman town and fort. Attacked unsuccessfully by Glyn Dwr in 1401, 1403-5.

Caerphilly Castle, South Wales. Begun in 1268 by Gilbert de Clare as a stronghold against Llywelyn the Great who destroyed it in 1270; rebuilt after 1271. Glyn Dwr attacked both castle and town. Cromwell's troops blasted the tower.

Carreg Cennen Castle, **Llandeilo**, South West Wales. Part of the old Kingdom of Deheubarth and the Lord Rhys. 1403 attacked and besieged by Glyn Dwr; much damage done but not taken.

Castell Dinas Bran, **Llangollen**, North East Wales. Thirteenth century castle close to Abbey of Valle Crucis. Possibly besieged by Glyn Dwr, defended by Earl of Arundel or used by the Welsh during their campaign.

Castell Newydd Emlyn (Newcastle Emlyn) Castle, South West Wales. Built c1240 and attacked by Glyn Dwr with success in 1403.

Castell-y-Bere, **Abergynolwyn**, Mid Wales. Unlike Edward I's castles which were built either on the coast or on navigable rivers, this early Welsh castle guards the mountain passes which were more vital when the enemy came from inland. It was probably begun by Llywelyn the Great but was strengthened by Edward I after its capture by the Earl of Pembroke. Llywelyn the Last's brother, David, used Bere as a centre of resistance in 1282 but he was forced to flee and his garrison surrendered to the English. From the ruins there is a glorious view of Bird Rock and surrounding countryside.

Cefnllys Castle, **Llandrindod Wells**, Mid Wales Borderland. Listed as "defensible" in Henry IV's survey.

Chepstow Castle, South East Wales. Provided with a large garrison in 1403 although Glyn Dwr did not attack. The only Roman civil town of Caerwent is situated a few miles away. The Norman fortress is called Striguil.

Chirk Castle, North East Wales. Built during Edward I's campaigns and strengthened by Roger Mortimer, Earl of March.

Church of St Nicholas, **Montgomery**, Mid Wales Borderlands. Contains two medieval effigies, the smaller of which is believed to be that of Edmund Mortimer, Glyn Dwr's son-in-law.

Cilgerran Castle, West Wales. Thirteenth century castle ruins, Glyn Dwr's forces caused much damage.

Coity Castle, **Bridgend**, South Wales. Besieged by Glyn Dwr. House of Commons requested Henry IV to help free the Lord of Coity. Two other Norman castles, Ogmore Castle and New Castle, are close by.

Conwy Castle, North Wales. Built by Edward I, garrisoned in 1285. Richard II sought safety here on return from Ireland in 1399; visited by Northumberland who promised him safe conduct to London. In 1401 castle was seized by William and Rhys Tudor who tricked the inhabitants on Good Friday; pardoned by Hotspur who reclaimed Conwy for the king. It remained impregnable.

Corwen Church, North Wales. A rough cross cut over the South Porch is, traditionally, Owen Glyn Dwr's dagger mark. It has been suggested by one authority that the Welsh Prince was buried here in the peaceful graveyard close to his home.

Criccieth Castle, North West Wales. Built in time of Llywelyn the Great. Edward I held Llywelyn the Last there as a prisoner. Defences were strengthened by Prince Henry in 1402. Garrison was besieged and the castle was captured and destroyed by Glyn Dwr in 1404.

Cymmer Abbey, **Dolgellau**, Mid Wales. Founded in 1198-9, first Charter in 1209 granted by Llywelyn the Great. His cousins, Gruffydd and Maredudd, the sons of Cynan ap Owain Gwynedd, were the main benefactors as both had helped Llywelyn at the Battle of Conwy in 1194.

Denbigh Castle, North Wales. Edward I's reign castle built. 1402 town attacked and burnt by Glyn Dwr. Castle held by Hotspur – not attacked.

Dinas Powis Castle, South Wales. Eleventh century with thirteenth century additions. Attacked by Glyn Dwr 1403.

Dinefwr Castle, South West Wales. Early thirteenth century castle, possibly on site of earlier fortification of Rhodri Mawr. Present castle more recent.

Dolbadarn Castle, **Llanberis**, North West Wales. Ancient Welsh castle used by Llywelyn the Last. Possibly used by Glyn Dwr to imprison Lord Grey of Ruthin and other hostages.

Dryslwyn Castle, **Llandeilo**, South West Wales. Early Welsh castle, held in 1282 by the grandson of the Lord Rhys. Attacked by Glyn Dwr c1403. Close to Dinefwr Castle, the home of the Princes of South Wales, and Carreg Cennen.

Flint Castle, North East Wales. An Edward I castle. Richard II escorted to this stronghold to meet the usurper Henry Bolingbroke before his abdication and removal to Pontefract.

Grosmont Castle, South East Wales. An old border castle above the River Monnow, thirteenth century, built to protect the English frontier. Scene of defeat for the Welsh and a turning-point in the rebellion.

Harlech Castle, North West Wales. Site of the legendary Welsh castle, home of Bran and scene of tales in the *Mabinogion*. Present structure built by Edward I. Long siege 1404 ended in capture by the Welsh. Used as main base by Glyn Dwr, possibly as the seat of Parliament, but recaptured by Talbot in 1409 when Glyn Dwr's family taken prisoner.

Hay Castle, **Hay-on-Wye**, South East Wales. Glyn Dwr caused damage to the town and castle.

Hwifordd (Haverfordwest) Castle, West Wales. Thirteenth century town burnt by Llywelyn the Great in 1220, also by Glyn Dwr in 1405, but the castle not taken.

Kidwelly Castle, South West Wales. Built by the Bishop of Salisbury, defended by the Normans against the Princes of South Wales. Once belonged to John of Gaunt, then to Henry IV.

Laugharne Castle, South West Wales. Ancient castle of Welsh princes which was listed as "defensible" by Henry IV in 1403. Carew ambushed the Welsh from this base and Glyn Dwr was forced to withdraw.

Llanegryn Church, near Tywyn, Mid Wales. This contains what is believed to be the Rood Screen from Cymmer Abbey, transported here for safety at the Dissolution of the Monasteries. The church is delightfully situated in the region of Castell-y-Bere and reached by a narrow road from the village.

Llanfair-ym-Muallt (Builth), Mid Wales Borderlands. Built during the reign of Edward I but now ruined. Llywelyn the Last was killed close by at Aberedw and monument is at Cilmeri.

Llanstephan Castle, South West Wales. A twelfth/thirteenth century castle with large-scale building ordered by Edward I. Taken by the Welsh but re-taken for Henry in 1403.

Llanymddyfri (Llandovery), South West Wales. Norman castle attacked by the Welsh in 1403. King Henry rested here during the campaign and executed the "worthy squire of Caio".

Monmouth Castle, South East Wales. Prince Henry born here in 1387, and named Harry of Monmouth later to become Henry V. After Welsh defeat at Grosmont, Glyn Dwr retaliated by massacring English forces near here, pushing the survivors back into the town.

New Radnor Castle, Mid Wales Borderlands. Norman building greatly damaged by Glyn Dwr after Battle of Pilleth.

Penfro (Pembroke) Castle, West Wales. An eleventh century castle birth-place of Henry VII.

Picton Castle, **Hwiffordd** (Haverfordwest), West Wales. Norman castle with thirteenth and fourteenth century buildings added. Possibly suffered damage to the surrounding lands during the Welsh revolt and the French invasion.

Pilleth Church, near Tref-y-Clawdd (Knighton), Mid Wales Borderlands. The original belfry is intact although the main structure is recent. The Battle of Pilleth was fought mainly on the slopes behind the church and it is believed that many of the dead were buried either in the vicinity or in the churchyard itself. It is reached by a grass track from the road. The font is original fourteenth century.

Powis Castle, **U Trallwng** (Welshpool), Mid Wales Borderlands. Enlarged during the thirteenth century by Gwenwynwyn family. Earlier castle was on another site.

Rhuddlan Castle, North Wales. Eighth century foundations, then Norman, with Edward I extending building into fortress. Famous for the Statute of Rhuddlan.

Ruthin, North East Wales. Built by Edward I in 1282. Held by Lord Grey who was later captured, and ruined by Glyn Dwr, who demanded an exorbitant ransom. Town attacked and ravaged by Welsh rebels in 1400.

Sant Gedifail's Church, **Penmynydd**, North West Wales. A fourteenth century structure containing an alabaster tomb to Gronw ap Tudur and his wife Myfanwy, dated 1385, which was removed from the Friary at Llanfaes after the Dissolution. Tudor Chapel is a later addition.

Tenby Castle, West Wales. Welsh stronghold originally, captured by Normans. Became a non-Welsh-speaking settlement populated by Flemings who fought against Glyn Dwr.

Usk Castle, South East Wales. Built in the twelfth century and owned by the Clare family. Attacked periodically by Welsh forces without success.

White Castle, near **Abergavenny**, South East Wales. With Grosmont it formed a defensive line to protect the Marches. Once held by William de Braose. Extensions were completed in thirteenth century and it was granted to the King's elder son, the Lord Edward, later Edward I. In 1267 White, Grosmont and Skenfrith Castles were transferred to his younger brother Edmund Crouchback, Earl of Lancaster. Earlier name Llantilio Castle but by thirteenth century became White Castle, in Welsh, Castell Gwyn.

Wolf's Castle, West Wales. No site, but name given to village north of Hwiffordd in the vicinity of Treffgarne; possible birthplace of Owen Glyn Dwr.

APPENDIX III

Early Rulers — Wales.

- CUNEDDA Duke of Britain 5th century (from Northumbria)
  - Maelgwyn Gwynedd d.547 contemporary King Arthur
    - Cadwaladr
      - Idwal
        - Rhodri Molwynog
          - Conan Tindaethwy
            - Esyllt = Mervin
              - RHODRI MAWR, the Great (844-878)
                - ANARAWD 878-916*
                  - Idwal Foel, the Bald d.942
                    - Iago 950-979
                    - Ieuan
                      - HYWEL THE BAD 979-985
                        - CYNAN 999-1005
                      - CADWALLON 985-986
                    - Meurig d.986
                      - Idwal d.996
                        - Iago 1023-1039
                          - Cynan
                            - GRUFFYDD ap CYNAN 1081-1137
                              - Owain Gwynedd 1137-1170
                                - DAFYDD 1170-1194
                                - Iorwerth Drwyndwn
                                  - LLYWELYN FAWR the Great 1194-1240
                                    - Gruffydd
                                      - LLYWELYN ap GRUFFYDD the LAST. 1246-1282
                                        - Gwenllian
                                    - DAFYDD 1240-1246
                                    - Gladys Ddu, the Dark = Reginald de Braose (1) = Ralph Mortimer (2)
                                      - Roger Mortimer
                                        - Edmund Mortimer 1st Lord Mortimer
                                          - Roger Mortimer 1st Earl of March*
                - CADELL d.909
                  - HYWEL DDA, THE GOOD 916-950
                    - Owain d.988
                      - MAREDUDD 986-999
                        - Angharad ‡
                      - Einion d.984Ø

*See Gwynedd. ‡ see Powys Øsee Dcheubarth (2)

The Line of Descent: GWYNEDD, North Wales.

RHODRI MAWR (844-878)

ANARAWD 878-916 — CADELL*

Idwal Foel d.942

IAGO 950-979 — IEUAN — MEURIG

(IEUAN) Hywel — Cadwallon

Hywel: Cynan

(MEURIG) Idwal

Iago

Cynan

GRUFFYDD ap CYNAN 1081-1137

OWAIN GWYNEDD 1137-1170

Dafydd 1170-1194 — Iorwerth Drwyndwn

(Iorwerth Drwyndwn) LLYWELYN FAWR THE GREAT 1194-1240

Gruffydd — DAFYDD 1240-1246 — Gladys Ddu the Dark = 1. Reginald de Braose = 2.Ralph Mortimer

(Gruffydd) LLYWELYN ap GRUFFYDD the LAST 1246-1282

(Ralph Mortimer) Roger Mortimer

Edmund Mortimer 1st Lord Mortimer

Roger Mortimer 1st Earl of March

Sir Edmund Mortimer

Roger Mortimer

Edmund Mortimer

Roger Mortimer 4th Earl of March

Anne married RICHARD, Earl of Cambridge

*See Deheubarth (1) and (2) †See Deheubarth (1)

The Line of Descent: POWYS

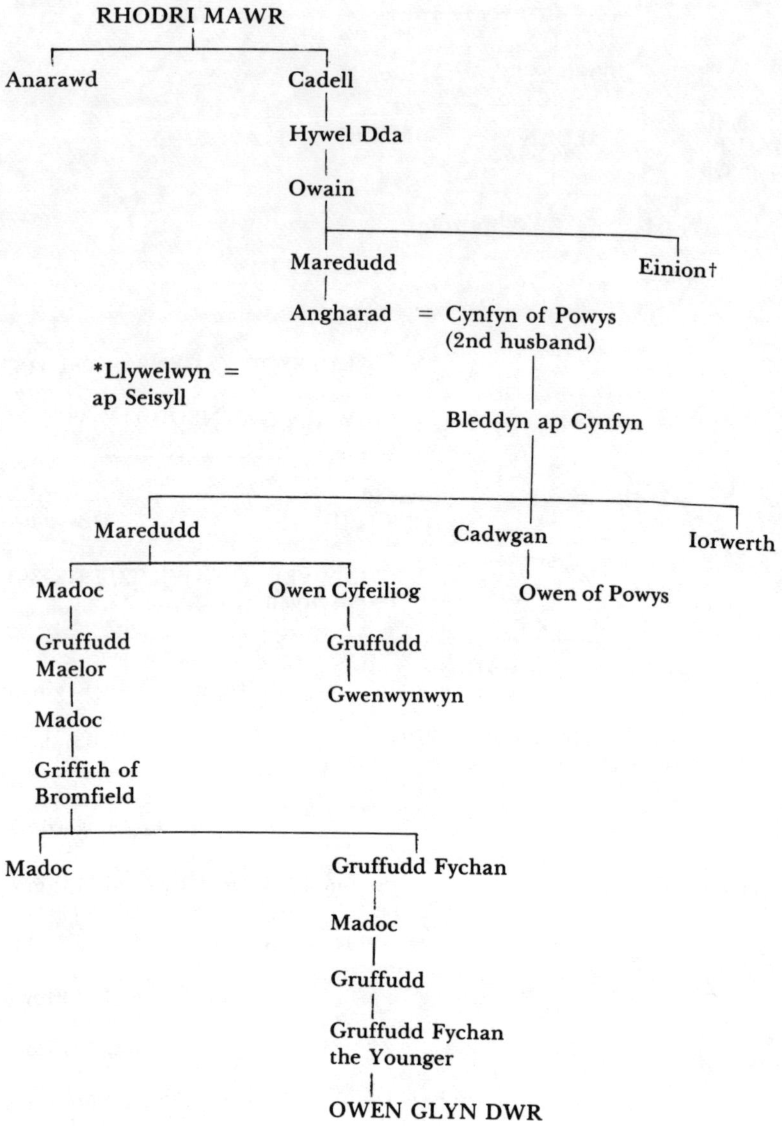

*See Deheubarth (1)
†See Deheubarth (2)

The Line of Descent DEHEUBARTH (1) South Wales

RHODRI MAWR (the Great) 844-878

Anarawd

CADELL d.909

Hywel Dda (the Good) 916-950

Owain

Maredudd 986-999

Einion †

Llywelyn ap Seisyll = Angharad = secondly Cynfyn of Powys

Gruffydd ap Llywelwyn 1039-1063

BLEDDYN 1063-1075

Nest (heir) = Osbern Fitz Richard

Nest (heir) = Bernard of Neufmarche

Sybil (heir) = Miles of Gloucester

Bertha (co-heir) = William de Braose

REGINALD DE BRAOSE = GLADYS DDU (the Dark) = secondly
daughter of Llywelyn the Great

RALPH MORTIMER*

William de Braose

MAUD (co-heir) = ROGER MORTIMER

Edmund Mortimer
1st Lord Mortimer

ELIZABETH OF YORK (heir)
= HENRY TUDOR, Henry VII

*See Gwynedd
†See Deheubarth (2)

The Line of Descent: DEHEUBARTH (2) South Wales

- RHODRI MAWR (the Great) 844-878
  - Anarawd*
  - CADELL d.909
    - Hywel Dda (the Good) 916-950
      - Owain d.988
        - Maredudd
          - Angharad†
        - Einion d.984
          - Cadell
            - Tewdwr Mawr
              - RHYS ap TEWDWR d.1093
                - Gruffydd d.1137
                  - Rhys ap Gruffydd the Lord Rhys d.1197
                    - Gwenllian = EDNYFED FYCHAN
                      - Goronwy
                        - TUDOR HEN d.1311
                          - Goronwy ap Tudor d.1331
                            - Sir Tudor Vychan of Penmynydd, Anglesey
                              - Maredudd ap Tudor
                                - Owen Tudor d.1461 = Catherine of France (Widow of Henry V)
                                  - Edmund Tudor Earl of Richmond = Margaret Beaufort
                                    - HENRY TUDOR, HENRY VII of England
                                  - Jasper Earl of Pembroke
                                  - Owen (a monk)
                                  - Margaret (died).

*See Gwynedd †See Powys and Deheubarth (1)

APPENDIX IV

The Tribal System, the Hall and the Lord Rhys.

Isle of Anglesey: the island was divided into three CANTREFS, and each cantref was divided into two CYMWDS. Each cantref contained a MANOR, or chieftain's residence which formed the centre for the dependent VILLAE or hamlets scattered over the two cymwds.

e.g. The Manor of Aberffraw.

The Free Tenants: the WELE, or GWELY, was a family or kindred group, occupying a hamlet, therefore several WELES lived in one hamlet. By the late thirteenth century, the old food-rents of the Weles had been commuted in to money payments, as rents. Other services were required from the Free Tenants, each man working according to his talents: the carpenter was not liable for work on hawking expeditions.

The MAERDREF was the Prince's home farm, worked by the VILLANI, the "unfree" tenants who had also to supply the wants of the Prince and his household.

e.g. 9 Villani had to supply—the milk of 3 cows; 4½ sheep; 9 lambs; 150 eggs, 27 hens etc.

another 6 Villani: 27 hens plus three day's work cutting corn. They also supplied fire and straw in the Royal Court. 600 day-works of men and horses were due to complete harrowing.

These services were due from groups of holdings and were not charges upon single occupants.

In each cantref, or cymwd, was a manor with its courts, forming a centre for legal proceedings, where dues were paid and services agreed. All the VILLAE or hamlets within the cantref were under the jurisdiction of its courts. The dues and services of both Free and Villein hamlets were regarded not as personal services, but as attached to particular HOLDINGS or hamlets; thus they remained unchanged either by confiscations or depopulation. They continued exactly the same for centuries.

The fully freeborn BONEDDIG of pure Welsh blood, both on his father's side and on his mother's side belonged to a KINDRED, and the Cymric tribe was a "bundle" of such kindreds bound together by common interests and frequent intermarriages. The whole tribe or country, the GWLAD, under the head king was regarded as the supreme kindred. Thus the descendants of a common ancestor to the NINTH degree were members of one kindred group.

The brenhin's Hall: the Hall could be constructed quickly, and may have been used for only one or two nights, yet, it was soundly built and would have stood firm for longer periods if required. Sometimes the "king's" men built more than one main structure if there was a large number to accommodate, rather like a portable village. Should the leader use the area frequently, for hunting, then the Hall would be used many times, with the minimum re-furbishing and re-thatching.

Six hefty poles, or trees, were placed in two parallel lines of three, fastened at the top to the roof-tree to form a nave. Behind the poles, low walls of stakes and wattle shut in the aisles. The roof was of branches and thatch; the doors were of wattle. Along the aisles were beds of rushes, and the footboards of the beds were used as seats in the day-time.

There was a fire in the middle, between the central posts, which divided the upper portion of the Hall, separating the chief and his officers from the humbler retainers who used the other end. The only decorations were the weapons of the men, which were hung on the walls in readiness, and, occasionally, curtains or 'rough hangings which thwarted some of the draughts which penetrated the wattle hurdles.

Trees, branches and turves were easily gathered and in plentiful supply, so the "king" could move around his district as he pleased. Game was abundant, and this rather nomadic existence ensured that any particular area was not exposed to excessive hunting.

The Lord Rhys:

1176—And the Lord Rhys held a grand festival at the castle of Aberteifi wherein he appointed two sorts of contention; one between the bards and poets, and the other between the harpers, fiddlers, pipers and various performers of instrumental music; and he assigned two chairs for the victors in the contentions; and these he enriched with vast gifts. A young man of his own court, son of Cibon the fiddler, obtained the victory in instrumental song; and the men of Gwynedd obtained the victory in vocal song; and all the other minstrels obtained from the Lord Rhys as much as they asked for, so that there was no one excluded. And that festival was proclaimed a year before it was held, throughout Wales and England and Prydyn and Ireland and many other countries.

from: BRUT y TYWYSGOGION THE CHRONICLE OF THE PRINCES:

Published by the Lords Commissioners of Her Majesty's Treasury under the direction of the Master of the Rolls. 1860

Books for Further Reading

A History of Wales, Vol. 1 and Vol. 2. J. E. Lloyd.
The History of Wales. Owen Edwards.
The Tribal System in Wales. Frederic Seebohm.
Feudal Britain. G. W. S. Barrow.
The Middle Ages. W. F. Bolton.
The Later Middle Ages. George Holmes.
Henry V. Peter Earle.
The Pelican History of England [4]. A. R. Myers.
The Pelican History of Medieval Europe. Maurice Keen.
A History of Europe. H. A. L. Fisher.
Brut y Tywysogion—The Chronicle of the Princes.
The Merioneth Lay Subsidy Roll (1292-3). K. Williams-Jones.
A History of the English Language. Albert C. Baugh.
A First Sketch of English Literature. Henry Morley.
Shakespeare's History Plays. E. M. W. Tillyard.
William Shakespeare. A. L. Rowse.
Owen Glendower [Owen Glyn Dwr]. J. E. Lloyd.
Owen Glyndwr. A. G. Bradley.
North Wales. Edited by H. L. V. Fletcher.
A Book of Wales. Edited by D. M. & E. M. Lloyd.
Poems of Wales. Selected by Edmund D. Jones.
Richard II. William Shakespeare.
Henry IV, Part One. William Shakespeare.
Henry IV, Part Two. William Shakespeare.
Henry V. William Shakespeare.
Richard III. William Shakespeare.
The Canterbury Tales. Geoffrey Chaucer.
The Anglo-Saxon Chronicle. Translated by G. N. Garmonsway.
The History of the Kings of Britain. Geoffrey of Monmouth.
The Journey through Wales. Gerald of Wales.
Sir Gawain and the Green Knight. (Penguin Classics).
The Castles of Wales. Alan Reid.
The Royal Line of Succession. Edited by Patrick W. Montague-Smith.
Castle and Historic Places in Wales. Wales Tourist Board.
Welsh Literature: (in translation)
The Mabinogion.
A Manual of Welsh Literature. J. C. Morrice.

Other:

Il Principe (The Prince). N. Macchiavelli.
The Divine Comedy. Dante (Translated by Dorothy L. Sayers).

Maps:
Ordnance Survey Routemaster Series, Sheet 7, Wales and West Midlands (about 1 inch to 4 miles).
Wales Tourist Board, Wales Tourist Map (1 inch to 5 miles).

Index